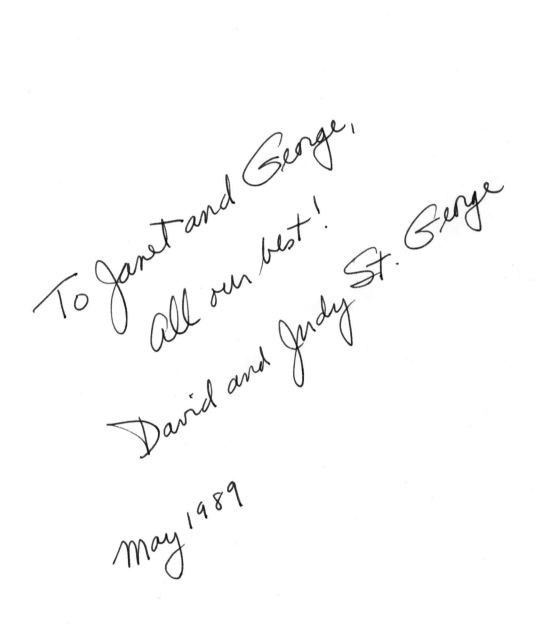

To Janet and George,
All our best!

David and Judy St. George

May 1989

PANAMA CANAL

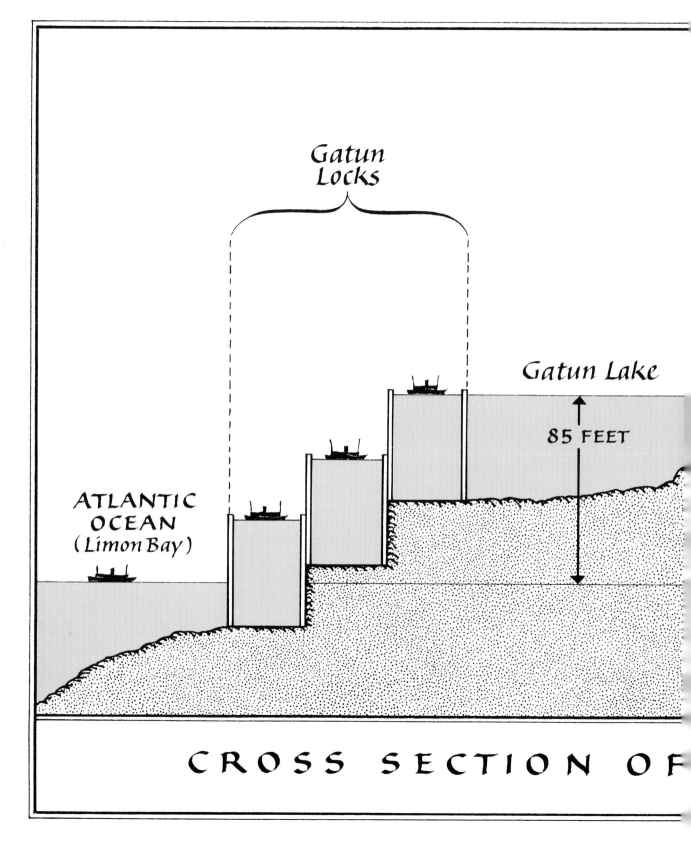

Gatun
Locks

Gatun Lake

85 FEET

ATLANTIC
OCEAN
(Limon Bay)

CROSS SECTION OF

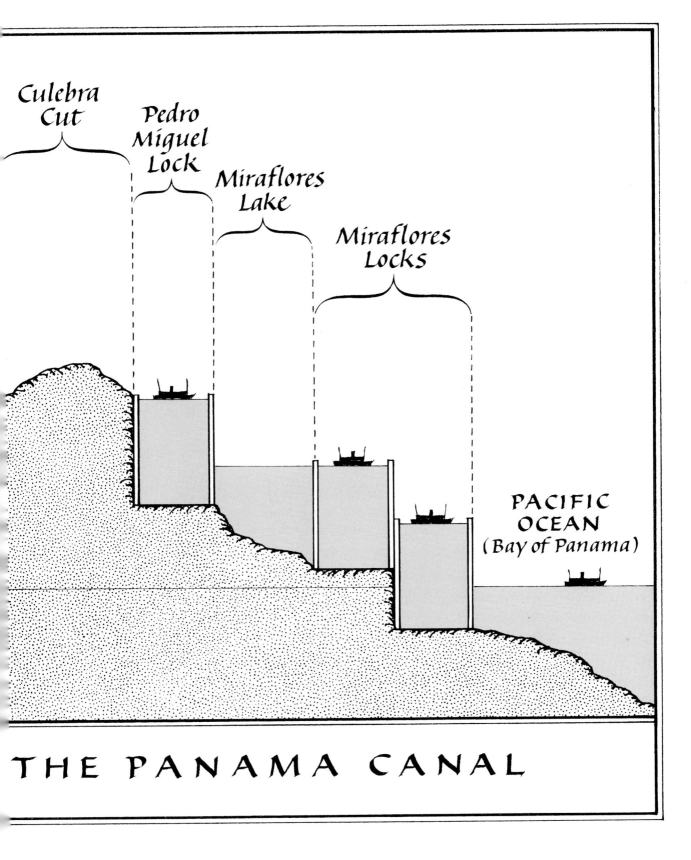

Culebra Cut

Pedro Miguel Lock

Miraflores Lake

Miraflores Locks

PACIFIC OCEAN
(Bay of Panama)

THE PANAMA CANAL

PANAMA

GATEWAY TO THE WORLD

CANAL

JUDITH ST. GEORGE

illustrated with photographs

G.P. Putnam's Sons · New York

To my fellow-researcher, photographer and
companion on this journey across the Isthmus,
my husband David

Copyright © 1989 by Judith St. George
All rights reserved.
Published simultaneously in Canada
Printed in the United States of America
First Impression
Book design by Christy Hale

Library of Congress Cataloging-in-Publication Data
St. George, Judith.
Panama canal: gateway to the world/
Judith St. George: illustrated with photographs. p.   cm.
Summary: Presents a history of the Panama Canal
from the time Columbus first anchored off the coast
of Panama through the signing of the 1977
United States-Panama treaties.
ISBN 0-399-21637-5
1. Panama Canal (Panama)—History—Juvenile
literature. [1. Panama Canal (Panama)—History.]
I. Title. F1569.C2S74   1988
972.87′5—dc19   88-11617   CIP   AC

ACKNOWLEDGMENTS

To all those who helped me research this book, I'd especially like to thank the Panama Canal Commission staff who not only made their resources available, but also arranged a transit of the canal during a particularly stressful time in Panama. My thanks to Willie K. Friar, Deputy Director of Public Affairs, Diane Morris, Nan S. Chong, Librarian of the Panama Canal Collection Library, Irene de Gonzalez of the Technical Resources Center, Cleveland C. Soper, Chief of the Graphic Branch and Paul N. Reid.

The New York Public Library's helpful and knowledgeable Science Division staff, as well as the library's complete collection of Panama Canal books, notebooks, reports, plans, diagrams, historical accounts and the *Canal Record* made the writing of this book possible. The National Archives Still Picture Branch Division and the Library of Congress staffs were also unfailingly helpful.

My husband, David, to whom this book is dedicated, was of incalculable assistance in every phase of research and writing. His eye for technical detail was particularly valuable to my understanding of the engineering section. My thanks.

One

It didn't seem possible that President Theodore Roosevelt was actually going to Panama. After all, no president serving in office had ever left the United States before and yet here was the president planning to travel all the way to Central America to check on how work was going on *his* Panama Canal. Still, it had been two years since construction had begun and everyone knew that Roosevelt considered the canal a top priority of his presidency.

On November 9, 1906, President Roosevelt, his wife, doctor and three Secret Service men set sail for Panama on the U.S.S. *Louisiana,* the largest battleship in the American fleet. Because the president wasn't expected to dock until November 15, the welcoming committee panicked when the *Louisiana* arrived in Panama a day early. President and Mrs. Roosevelt's hotel rooms still weren't ready. Fortunately, Roosevelt sent word that they would spend the night on the *Louisiana.*

But while the welcoming committee (and the Secret Service)

were eating an early breakfast the next morning at the hotel, President Roosevelt came ashore. Frank Maltby, who was on the canal staff, described the president's arrival: "Around the point came a Naval launch carrying the Presidential flag, an hour ahead of time, with no one on hand to greet or salute the great man. He climbed up onto the dock and walked about talking to the carpenters."

Roosevelt's unannounced arrival gave the canal staff a taste of the three days to come. As Maltby told the story, Roosevelt disappeared that first morning soon after he reached his hotel. "He bolted out the back door, rushed up the hill to the Hospital and into the wards, where he began talking to the patients as to their

President [in middle] and Mrs. Roosevelt tour the canal in a special railroad car during their 1906 trip to Panama.

treatment and care. No one knew he was there until a nurse came in." By early afternoon the president had not only inspected the hospital but had also toured the bay in a tugboat and eaten a thirty-cent lunch at an employees' dining hall where he and Mrs. Roosevelt had showed up unexpectedly while the official banquet went on without them.

It was typical of Roosevelt that he had chosen to visit Panama in the middle of the rainy season. He wanted to see work on the canal under the most difficult conditions and his wish was granted. He later wrote to his son Kermit, "For two days there [were] uninterrupted tropic rains without a glimpse of the sun . . . so that we saw the climate at its worst. It was just what I desired to do."

As others fell by the wayside, Roosevelt kept up his usual strenuous pace. "I tramped everywhere through the mud," he wrote Kermit. And he did. He hiked along the railroad tracks, leaped ditches, made speeches, talked to workers and inspected living quarters from top to bottom, including the outhouses. Maltby later said about Roosevelt, "He was continually pointing to some feature and asking, 'What's that?' 'That is so-and-so.' 'Well, I want to see it.'" When Roosevelt decided to watch construction from a hilltop, he gave the order, Maltby said, and "we, together with three or four secret service men, charged up the hill as if we were taking a fort by storm."

On the second day of his visit, three inches of rain fell in two hours, the worst downpour in fifteen years. The rain didn't bother Roosevelt a bit. While traveling along the canal route by train, he spotted several steam shovels excavating for the channel. He ordered the train to stop, got out, slogged through the mud, climbed up onto the driver's seat of one of the mammoth steam shovels and asked the driver to show him how it worked. An obviously delighted president was at the controls for about twenty minutes

President Roosevelt sits at the controls of a 95-ton steam shovel on the second day of his visit to Panama.

while the torrential rains soaked everyone, including Roosevelt, who was dressed all in white.

By the time the president and his party sailed from Panama after their three-day visit, the canal staff was exhausted and waterlogged. "I have blisters on both my feet and am worn out," complained the chief engineer.

On shipboard, Roosevelt wrote to Kermit describing work on the canal: ". . . the huge shovels are hard at it; scooping huge masses of rock and gravel and dirt. . . . They are eating steadily into the mountain, cutting it down and down." He added, "It [Panama] is a real tropic forest, palms and bananas, breadfruit trees, bamboos and gorgeous butterflies and brilliant colored birds fluttering among the orchids. There are beautiful flowers, too."

If President Roosevelt was aware of the conflict between Panama's unique tropical beauty and the raw and muddy wound that was being dug across its landscape, he never mentioned it. But then, few others had either, for ever since the first European explorers landed in Panama, its history has been one of exploitation and plunder.

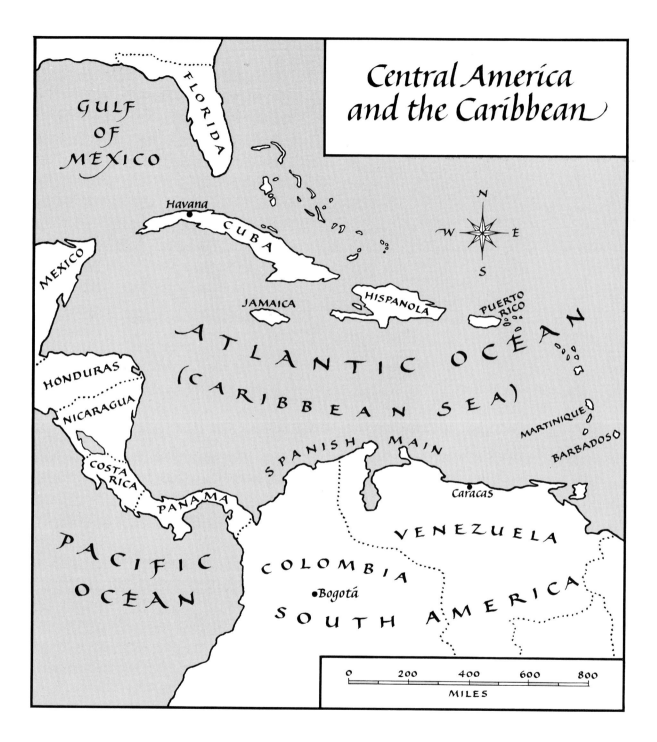

Central America
and the Caribbean

GULF
OF
MEXICO

FLORIDA

Havana

CUBA

MEXICO

JAMAICA

HISPANOLA

PUERTO
RICO

ATLANTIC OCEAN
(CARIBBEAN SEA)

HONDURAS

NICARAGUA

MARTINIQUE

BARBADOS

COSTA
RICA

SPANISH MAIN

PANAMA

Caracas

PACIFIC
OCEAN

VENEZUELA

COLOMBIA

•Bogotá

SOUTH AMERICA

0   200   400   600   800

MILES

Two

It didn't take long for the world to realize that Panama is the narrowest strip of land between the Atlantic and Pacific oceans. From the early sixteenth century, explorers, conquerors, treasure seekers, settlers, the military and engineers have descended on Panama to find a route that would join the two oceans, build their own route or seize one that already existed. A modern-day Panamanian anthropologist says, ''A road, a railroad, or a canal; they didn't concern themselves with the rest. That's been the story here for hundreds of years.''

Christopher Columbus, who believed that he was in Southeast Asia, was searching for a water route to India when he anchored off the Atlantic coast of Panama. The year was 1502 and his anchorage was near where Rodrigo de Bastidas, the first white man to set foot in Panama, had anchored the year before. But as soon as Columbus saw the gold ornaments and nose rings that the natives wore, he decided to stay a while and establish a trading post. Columbus's son Ferdinand later wrote that the friendly and curious natives who had immigrated thousands of years before from either South America or the West Indies were "the best favored Indians the Christians had yet seen, being tall and spare, not potbellied, and handsome of face."

But from the time of their first encounter with white men, the natives' days were numbered. In their pursuit of "gold, glory and gospel" (mostly gold), the Spanish almost completely destroyed Panama's native population by sword, disease and slavery. But in 1510 a Spaniard arrived in Panama who was less interested in gold than he was in finding the sea that natives told him lay to the south. Vasco Núñez de Balboa was described as "thirty-five years of age, tall, well-shap'd and limb'd, strong, of a good Aspect, fair-hair'd, ingenious, and patient under Hardship." Accompanied by 190 Spanish army volunteers, 800 natives and a pack of hounds, Balboa marched into Panama's steaming jungle on September 1, 1513. Four weeks later, he climbed to the top of a mountain, gazed to the south and then fell to his knees in prayer. He had sighted

A romantic version of Balboa sighting the Pacific Ocean, September 1513.

The Royal Road built by the Spanish in the 16th century is the first land route to join the Atlantic and Pacific oceans.

the Pacific Ocean. The world, not to mention Panama, would never be the same again.

Some twenty years later, the Spanish completed a seven-foot-wide road across Panama, known as the Royal Road, over which they transported the thousands of tons of gold and silver that they plundered from Peru and Mexico. The treasure was landed by ship on the Pacific coast at the city of Old Panamá, where it was loaded first on muletrains and then on riverboats for the fifty-mile journey across Panama to the Atlantic coast. There it was transferred to galleons for the voyage back to Spain.

As early as 1529, a Spanish priest, Alvaro de Saavedra, drew up plans for a canal route across Panama. Spanish royalty was interested in a canal, too, with sixteenth-century Spanish kings ordering surveys of possible Central American routes. Perhaps one reason that nothing ever came of the surveys was that by 1550 the Spanish conquerors, known as the conquistadores, controlled all the Caribbean Sea (part of the Atlantic Ocean) and Central America, as well as land in South America. Understandably, they weren't very enthusiastic about building a canal that would open the riches of the New World to other nations.

But not even a world power like Spain could keep such wealth to herself, and for the next one hundred years a vicious band of English, French and Dutch seamen known as buccaneers terrorized Spanish shipping in the Caribbean and that section of ocean off the coasts of Venezuela and Colombia that was known as the Spanish Main. Two of the most notorious buccaneers were Sir Francis Drake and Sir Henry Morgan, both of whom ambushed muletrains on the Royal Road, as well as looted and sacked Panama's main coastal cities and their treasuries. Because the buccaneers plundered, killed and burned with such brutality, Spain and England, longtime enemies, signed a treaty in 1670 in order to defend their interests in the New World mutually.

The newfound peace not only allowed the native Indian population to make a gradual comeback, but it also brought settlers, the most famous being a Scottish colony led by William Patterson that settled on Panama's Atlantic coast in 1698. Patterson hoped to open free trade between the Atlantic and Pacific over the same route that Balboa had taken across Panama almost two hundred years before. But as with other colonies, both before and since, disease, starvation and Spanish attacks so devastated the settlement that it didn't even last two years.

Considering that a passageway across Central America would shorten the sailing distance between the east and west coasts of the United States by almost 8,000 miles, as well as eliminate the dangerous journey around the tip of South America, all sorts of Central American passageways between the Atlantic and the Pacific were proposed in the early 1800s. The famous explorer Alexander von Humboldt designed plans for a canal as early as 1811 but technical know-how was too far in the future even to attempt it.

And then, in 1848, gold was discovered in California. Instead of traveling across the United States, many gold rushers sailed to the Atlantic coast of Panama and from there trekked across Panama on the old Royal Road to the Pacific, where they picked up another ship bound for California. Although it was only fifty miles across Panama, rain, heat, humidity, mud, wild animals and most of all, fever and sickness exacted a dreadful toll. One young man wrote back to his family, "I say it in fear of God and love of man, to one and all, for no consideration come this route."

The warnings didn't matter. The gold rushers continued to sail to Panama in such numbers that businessmen back in New York City decided an American railroad across Panama might be very profitable indeed. By 1850, workers, most of whom were West Indian descendants of African slaves imported by the Spanish during the 1500s and 1600s, were hacking their way through the jungle near Colón.

Living and working conditions were miserable. "It was a virgin swamp interlaced with huge vines and thorny shrubs," wrote an American engineer. "In the black slimy mud of its surface alligators and other reptiles abounded, while the air was laden with pestilential vapors and swarming with sandflies and mosquitoes."

During the five years it took to build the railroad, some 6,000 workers died from malaria, cholera, dysentery, yellow fever and smallpox. An unknown number of Chinese committed suicide from the "melancholia," an aftereffect of malaria. In 1852, the worst year of all, only two out of fifty American technicians survived.

Finally, in 1855, the one-track railroad that ran forty-seven and a half miles from Colón to Panama City was completed. The railroad had cost $8 million, more than any other railroad ever built, but with an unheard-of fare of twenty-five dollars in gold for one-way, it earned profits of more than $7 million in its first

six years. "This goose began to lay golden eggs with astonishing extravagance," was how one writer described its immediate success. Only when a transcontinental railroad across the United States was finished in 1869 were the Panama Railroad's golden-egg days at an end.

Still, talk of a Central American canal persisted and between 1870 and 1875, seven American surveys were made of possible routes, mostly by the U.S. Navy. The Frenchman Ferdinand de Lesseps, who had just finished building the Suez Canal in Egypt, was interested in building a Panamanian canal, too. "You succeeded at Suez by a miracle," de Lesseps's son warned his seventy-four-year-old father. "Should not one be satisfied with accomplishing one miracle in a lifetime?"

In reply, de Lesseps formed a canal company in 1879 naming himself as president. Under de Lesseps's leadership, the company bought the Panama Railroad from the United States for some $20 million and signed an agreement with Colombia to build a canal across Colombia's province of Panama. To prove to the world that he was healthy, vigorous and completely in charge, de Lesseps sailed to Panama for a month's stay with his beautiful second wife and several of his young children. A staff member, greatly impressed by de Lesseps, wrote, "Nothing ever seemed for an instant to dampen the ardor of his enthusiasm."

But de Lesseps had seen Panama in the dry season and soon after work began on the canal in 1881, the rainy season began, bringing with it torrential rains and the "sickly season." Nothing much had changed over the centuries. A French engineer described conditions: "The Isthmus is a damp tropical jungle, intensely hot, swarming with mosquitoes, snakes, alligators, scorpions, and centipedes; the home, even as Nature made it, of yellow fever, typhus and dysentery."

(Left) The newly completed Panama Railroad steams through Culebra as the villagers run from their huts to watch.

Ferdinand de Lesseps poses with his young wife and nine of their twelve children at the time of his first visit to Panama.

By September 1883, with steam shovels doing the heavy excavation work and approximately 10,000 men, mostly blacks from Jamaica and other West Indian islands, wielding picks, shovels and wheelbarrows, some progress was being made. But at a terrible price. In 1884 the French chief engineer estimated that of every one hundred arrivals, at least twenty died, and of those who survived, only about twenty were well enough to work. "It did not matter any difference whether they were black or white, to see the way they died there. They die like animals," a West Indian worker said years later.

By 1885 only ten percent of the work was finished and by December 1888, disease, deaths, inadequate equipment, technical problems, bad management and lack of money had bankrupted the company. Perhaps the biggest stumbling block of all had been de Lesseps's insistence on building a sea-level canal like his Suez Canal. He simply didn't understand that Suez's flat desert terrain made a sea-level canal possible (a sea-level canal simply diverts water into a wide ditch or channel without the need for locks or tunnels), while Panama's dense jungles, rivers and mountain ranges demanded a lock canal that could raise or lower boats from one level to another. With all work brought to a standstill, the estimated 16,000 deaths seemed particularly senseless. De Lesseps himself never recovered from the blow, living in seclusion until his own death in 1894.

France almost didn't recover either. In 1892 an official investigation into the canal company opened a Pandora's box of corruption, fraud, bribery and graft at all political and financial levels that destroyed countless reputations and toppled the French government. Although a new French canal company continued work in a half-hearted way until a buyer could be found for the property, to all intents and purposes, French hopes for a canal in Panama were finished forever. If nothing else, a lesson had been learned. An engineering project of this magnitude was too complex to be tackled by a private company. This was a job for a nation.

Three

Right from the beginning of his presidency, Teddy Roosevelt wanted a canal in Panama that would join the Atlantic and Pacific. "No single great material work which remains to be undertaken on this continent is of such consequence to the American people," he announced in his first address to Congress. The date was December 3, 1901, only two and a half months after President William McKinley had died from an assassin's bullet and Vice President Roosevelt had been sworn in as president.

The turn of the century was a time of optimism and growth, when the United States annexed Hawaii and acquired the Philippines, Guam and Puerto Rico after winning the Spanish American War in 1898 (Roosevelt and his Rough Riders had emerged from the war as heroes). At home, electricity, the telephone and the automobile were closing distances from coast to coast and with the western frontier settled, the expansion-minded Roosevelt dreamed of a canal linking the two oceans. "I wish to see the United States the dominant power on the shores of the Pacific Ocean," he declared.

By 1902, Congress, the military, business people and the public were pressing for a canal, too . . . in Nicaragua. After all, Nicaragua was closer to the United States than Panama, it had fewer engineering problems, its political situation was more stable and its climate was healthier. And look what had happened to the French in Panama!

But Roosevelt wanted Panama and with his usual determination, he put the full force of his extraordinary personality behind the fight. Finally, after weeks of debate, on June 26, 1902 Congress passed the Spooner Bill authorizing an American canal in Panama. Congress's decision had been influenced not only by the president but also by a special committee's recommendation and testimony by professional engineers . . . not to mention a recent volcanic eruption on a nearby West Indian island that had killed 25,000 people. After all, Nicaragua had nine active volcanoes while Panama had none.

Actually, geologists believe that much of Central America was once a chain of volcanic islands that gradually rose from the sea millions of years ago. Over time, as more and more lava poured down the mountains, the islands began to join together. Wind and rain deposited soil and rocks on the slopes so that a land bridge, or isthmus, was formed that connected North and South America. (An isthmus is any narrow strip of land connecting two larger bodies of land.)

Panama, somewhat smaller than the state of South Carolina, is the narrowest part of that isthmus, 480 miles long and anywhere from 30 to 120 miles wide, a total of nearly 30,000 square miles of mostly hilly and mountainous countryside. Situated directly south of Florida, Panama, which is often simply called the Isthmus, is shaped like an S lying on its back so that the Atlantic Ocean lies to its north and the Pacific Ocean to its south. Amazingly enough, from some parts of Panama, it is possible to watch the sun rise in the Pacific and set in the Atlantic. During Panama's May-to-December rainy season, the Pacific coast averages about 70 inches of rain, while only 50 miles or so away, the Atlantic coast gets as much as 130 inches.

The present population of Panama, an Indian word meaning "abundance of fish," is something over two million, with more than half the people living either in the capital, Panama City, which is on the Pacific coast, or in Colón on the Atlantic coast. Most of the rural population lives in small towns or farms scattered across western Panama, while eastern Panama's rain forest is sparsely settled by Indians. As ferociously dense as it was when Balboa and his soldiers struggled through it in 1513, Panama's rain forest is the only section of the Pan-American Highway from Alaska to the tip of South America that has not yet been completed.

The majority of Panamanians are Roman Catholic, either of mixed Spanish and Indian blood (known as mestizos) or mixed Spanish, Indian and West Indian blood. Although Spanish is the official language, with English a common second language, several Indian languages are spoken, too. Rich in folklore, music, dance and native Indian art, Panama is known especially for the elaborately embroidered molas that have been the Cuna Indians' traditional dress for generations.

Although Panama won its independence from Spain in 1821, it had voluntarily annexed itself to Colombia that same year so that in spite of countless uprisings and rebellions, in 1902 Panama remained a province of Colombia. Like President Roosevelt, the people of Panama were enthusiastic about having a canal across their country, but because they were still a province of Colombia, they were powerless to do anything about it.

Unable to deal directly with Panama, the United States began treaty talks with Colombia in 1902 to build a canal in Panama. Although a treaty was finally signed between the United States and Colombia in 1903 and ratified by the United States Senate, the Colombian Senate refused to approve it. The American representative in Colombia's capital city of Bogotá reported that Colombian newspapers were filled with "bitter hostility" toward "the attempt of a stronger nation to take advantage of Colombia and rob her of one of the most valuable sources of wealth which the world contains."

President Roosevelt was equally furious. In August 1903, he wrote a letter to his Secretary of State, John Hay, (marked personal) that expressed his feelings only too clearly: "I do not think that the Bogotá lot of jack rabbits should be allowed permanently to bar one of the future highways of civilization."

By September, Panamanian patriots had become increasingly anxious to win their freedom so that they could negotiate their own treaty. Roosevelt was anxious for them to be free agents, too. "I should be delighted if Panama were an independent State, or if it made itself so at this moment," he wrote to a Cabinet member in a letter that was also marked personal.

And then, on November 3, 1903, in an almost musical-comedy series of events, the Panamanian revolution began, wholeheartedly supported by the United States government. An order from the Department of State to the Panama Railroad not to transport Colombian troops, as well as the presence of the American gunboat U.S.S. *Nashville* in Panama's harbor, with a second gunboat arriving two days later, was all that Panama needed to gain her

The presence of the American gunboat U.S.S. Nashville *in Colón harbor plays a key role in the Panamanian revolution.*

freedom in three short days. (Only one life was lost, a Chinese shopkeeper killed by a stray shot.) Incredibly, on November 6, 1903, almost as soon as the White House learned that Panama had declared her independence, Secretary of State Hay formally recognized the Republic of Panama.

An immediate outcry was raised all over the world against President Roosevelt's interference in Colombia's internal affairs through "gunboat diplomacy." American newspapers were equally critical, with one editorial calling Roosevelt and his advisors "the hustling youth who are now playing football with international law." The outcry was understandable. The United States had just violated the Bidlack Treaty that the United States and Colombia had signed in 1846 guaranteeing that the United States would protect Colombia's interests in Panama in exchange for free and open transit across Panama "from one sea to the other." (It was the Bidlack Treaty that had opened the way for American businessmen to build the Panama Railroad.)

Unquestionably, American intervention in Panama was probably *the* most controversial act of Roosevelt's presidency and for years he gave all sorts of excuses for what he'd done. He had only wanted to help the "downtrodden" Panamanians win their freedom; Colombia couldn't keep order on the Isthmus; the United States had been policing the Isthmus for Colombia for too long; Colombia had no right to block the construction of such an important canal; Colombians weren't capable of building a canal themselves.

Nevertheless, three years before the canal was finished, when he was no longer president, Roosevelt admitted in a speech, "I am interested in the Panama Canal because I started it. . . . I took the Canal Zone and let Congress debate and while the debate goes on the Canal does, too." Exaggeration or not, the statement "I took the Canal Zone" has served to extend the controversy right down to the present time.

On November 18, 1903, Secretary of State Hay and the Panamanian envoy to Washington, Philippe Bunau-Varilla (who hadn't even consulted with Panamanian leaders), signed a treaty with terms so favorable to the United States and so unfavorable to Panama that even Roosevelt's political enemies were impressed. One senator commented that the treaty "comes to us more liberal in its concessions to us and giving us more than anybody in this Chamber [the Senate] ever dreamed of having . . ."

The United States was given the right to construct a canal in Panama through a zone ten miles wide (five miles on either side of the canal) over which the United States would have as much power and authority as if it were sovereign over the territory. Panama, in turn, would have no sovereign rights, power or authority in this zone. Although the cities of Colón and Panama City were within Zone boundaries, neither was to be considered part of the Zone except for American control over their sanitation, sewerage, water supply and maintenance of public order. Four small islands in the Bay of Panama were granted to the United States; in addition, the United States had the right to take over any land or water "necessary and convenient" for the construction, maintenance, operation, sanitation or protection of the canal. In return for the use, occupation and control of this zone of land and water "in perpetuity" (forever), the United States guaranteed the Republic of Panama her independence.

Although Panamanian leaders were furious that such an unfavorable treaty had been signed without their approval (one writer quipped that "the whole thing was done between lunch and dinner"), they had no armed forces to repel a possible Colombian invasion nor was there any money in their treasury. The guarantee of American military protection and the offer of ten million American dollars for rights to build a canal, followed by a $250,000 annual payment after the first nine years, as well as the promise of an American demand for local goods and services once construction began, left Panamanians no choice. They ratified the treaty on December 2, 1903.

"The United States is none too popular at any point south of its own borders. It is at the one time hated and feared," a commentator wrote. Colombia was in such an uproar, there was rioting in Bogotá, with other Latin American countries unanimously expressing outrage that the United States, which had promised to protect Colombian rights in Panama, had actually prevented Colombia from putting down a revolution in one of her own provinces. Even though the United States apologized and awarded Colombia $25 million in 1921, Colombia wasn't willing to recognize the Republic of Panama formally until 1925.

Although there was a fierce and bitter debate in the Senate between those who opposed Roosevelt's actions and those who supported him, the Senate finally ratified the treaty with Panama on February 23, 1904. Immediately Roosevelt swung into action by signing a bill to pay the French $40 million for all their land, equipment and buildings, as well as rights to the Panama Railroad, the largest real estate deal ever made. Roosevelt next appointed a seven-man Isthmian Canal Commission to draw up policy for the canal and direct construction.

In June 1904, the Commission hired John Findley Wallace as chief engineer for $25,000 a year (only Roosevelt himself earned a higher government salary). At age fifty-one, Wallace was a respected civil engineer who had won national honors but who had no special qualifications to run the greatest engineering project ever undertaken. As a matter of fact, Wallace tended to be indecisive and unassertive, the kind of person who was so consumed by details that he had trouble seeing the overall picture. What turned out to be even more of a problem was that Wallace had little ability for getting along with people.

John Findley Wallace is appointed chief engineer in June 1904.

On the other hand, the Commission's choice of Army doctor William C. Gorgas to head up all hospital and sanitary work was excellent. "You will take measures to secure the best medical experts for this purpose whom you can get," Roosevelt had told the Commissioners and they had. Gorgas was *the* leading American authority on tropical diseases. Meanwhile, Roosevelt appointed William Howard Taft, his new Secretary of War, to supervise the Commission and report directly back to him. Despite continuing criticism of his role in the Panama revolution, Roosevelt was impatient for work to start. "Tell them I am going to make the dirt fly!" he boasted.

On July 1, 1904, Chief Engineer Wallace arrived in Panama, followed shortly after by the seven members of the Commission. Although the Commissioners spent a month in the Canal Zone meeting every day with Wallace and touring the canal route, they didn't make any decisions. They didn't even decide whether the canal should be a lock canal or sea-level canal before they sailed for home to present glowing reports about Wallace to the president.

Another glowing report appeared in a magazine article written by a friend of Wallace's: "So pronounced and so extensive have been the improvements made by Chief Engineer Wallace in the past half year that they seem almost incredible." A medical note was added: "There is at the present time no more danger from yellow fever in Panama than there is from pneumonia and grippe in the United States."

Glowing reports or no glowing reports, reality on the Isthmus was far, far different.

Four

"**M**ake the dirt fly!" may have sounded good, but making the dirt fly in Panama was about the last thing that needed to be done. At this point, with still no decision made as to whether the canal should be lock or sea-level, chaos reigned. A New York editor wrote: "We have pitched in after the characteristic American way and hurried men and materials to the Isthmus without adequate wharfing facilities at either the Atlantic or Pacific ends, without quarters for the men, or storage for supplies. . . . The things ordered were not always right, and when they were, they did not arrive in right order."

And to say that Chief Engineer Wallace had been stunned by what he found on his arrival in Panama was an understatement. Canal headquarters were in Panama City, where the unpaved and unsewered streets were ankle-deep in foul mire during the rainy season and choking dust during the dry season, and where slops were routinely emptied on passersby from second-floor windows. Eighty French dredging machines had been sunk in the harbor and

A large tree has grown through an abandoned French dump car.

millions of dollars' worth of rusted French machinery was scattered from one end of the Canal Zone to the other, with only 700 men actually working. The barely functioning one-track Panama Railroad had worn-out equipment, filthy coaches, few signals or sidings and bridges that were in a state of collapse. Most of the 2,149 French buildings were half-hidden by jungle growth and ravaged by rats, termites and mold. A reporter summed up conditions: "We inherit a graveyard of many wrecked hopes and lives."

On the other hand, the French had excavated more than anyone had expected. They had left a water passage that began at the Atlantic entrance and ran eleven miles, with another channel running four and a half miles into the Bay of Panama in the Pacific, with excavation for thirty miles through the mountains. "One appreciated more and more the wonderful amount those French had really accomplished. . . . It touches from ocean to ocean," wrote a magazine correspondent.

At first Wallace viewed the situation as hopeless, but then six machine shops and a power plant were found to be in working order and hundreds of usable French tools, machines, engines and spare parts were discovered that had been safely stored away. Dredges and tugboats were raised from the harbor and rebuilt, while two excavators, a number of dump cars and locomotives, as well as other rusted and vine-covered equipment all proved to be worth repairing. Fifteen hundred of the French buildings were restored and eventually put to use, mostly as housing.

But the minute Wallace started to work on the canal, the Isthmian Canal Commission frustrated his every effort. Only one member, the Governor of the Panama Canal Zone, was even on the Isthmus, with the other six members 2,000 miles away in Washington waylaying every order and arguing over every dollar. With the French disaster fresh in their minds, they decided that there was no way they were going to be accused of the corruption and waste that symbolized the French effort to the world. The Commission chairman declared, ''Whether we build that canal or not we will leave things so fixed that those fellows up on the Hill [Congress] can't find anything in the shape of graft after us.''

Using that statement as its guideline, the tightfisted Commission tied work on the canal into knots. For each cart and wagon hired from the natives, the Commission demanded six government expense vouchers, while carpenters needed a signed permit to saw any boards that were over ten feet long. One order of supplies even arrived in tropical Panama complete with snow shovels. ''A requisition had to trudge from foreman to general foreman, to assistant superintendent, to superintendent, to Chief Engineer and be approved by each,'' a member of the Commission admitted later. Although mail between Panama and Washington took ten days by ship, to save money, all supervisors were told to mail their orders rather than wiring them by overseas cable.

When Wallace made plans to install water and sewer systems in Colón and Panama City, he cabled Washington for pipes in

August 1904. The Commission, arguing endlessly among themselves, finally put out bids for the pipes, which was followed by an automatic thirty-day waiting period. Wallace wired for the pipes again. And again. By the time the pipes began to arrive in January (by sailing schooner), the trenches dug for the pipes had all collapsed in the torrential rains of the rainy season. It didn't matter. The Commission hadn't shipped enough pipes anyway.

Commission policy wasn't the only bottleneck. Chief Engineer Wallace's approach to his job further hampered progress. When faced with the largest engineering project ever attempted, Wallace should have spent months, if not years, in preparation, making surveys, drawing up an overall plan, ordering and stockpiling supplies and equipment and especially seeing to the housing and feeding of the thousands of workers who would be needed. Last but not least, he should have tackled the problem of malaria and yellow fever. And when all the preparatory work was finished, Wallace should have presented his program to the Commission and insisted on its support.

But when Wallace traveled to Washington in September of 1904 to meet with President Roosevelt, Secretary of War Taft and the Commission, he apparently never made his demands known. He simply had no idea of how to go about the monumental job of organization, nor did he know how to get along with either those under him or those above him. He was almost never in contact with the work force, preferring to drive along the canal route in a small locomotive that the workers scornfully called "the Brain's Car." Furthermore, Wallace not only hated Panama, which he called this "God-forsaken country," but he was also terrified of disease. When he and his wife returned to Panama from the United States in November 1904, after a two-month stay, he brought along two expensive metal caskets . . . just in case.

Despite Wallace's lack of organization, he took Roosevelt's command to "make the dirt fly" seriously and started right in on the excavation work. Although Wallace's choice of the ninety-five-ton American Bucyrus steam shovels was first-rate, any excavation they accomplished was haphazard and basically useless. The Bucyrus shovels, which were three times the size of the French machines and more than three times as efficient, lay idle as often as not because there were no trains to carry away the dirt

In addition to the American steam shovels, Wallace tries to continue work with outdated French equipment.

and rocks that were being excavated. A magazine article described the scene: "Trains were blocked, the shovels stopped, men sat down and waited."

By November 1904, there were 3,500 employees in the Zone, all living under intolerable conditions. Although Americans had been promised clean, decent quarters with "a single bed, a mattress, a lamp, two chairs, a dresser, table, a washstand, and a bowl and pitcher," they found themselves on cots in filthy unscreened barracks, five or six to a room, with the food practically inedible and fresh eggs, milk, fruit and ice nonexistent. "The three things lacking to make life enjoyable on the Isthmus are all feminine," one magazine writer wisecracked, "women, cows, and hens." Another American commented, "The meals provided would sicken a dog." Even visitors were shocked. "We wondered how Americans of decent taste could stay more than six weeks in such a hole and keep their reason," one marveled.

Conditions were even worse for the West Indians who made up two-thirds of the work force. With almost no housing provided, they lived in the filthy slums of Colón or what shacks could be found or thrown together along the railroad line. "We had to bathe, wash our clothes in the same river; drink the same river water and cook with it," one worker recalled.

At the end of November 1904, Secretary Taft arrived in Panama for meetings with the Panamanian government, as well as to make an inspection tour of the Zone. Although his visit was a round of parties, banquets and picnics, when Taft returned to Washington, he reported to President Roosevelt that the project was far more difficult than anyone had imagined and that the Commission was obstructing all progress.

Roosevelt, who agreed with Taft, asked for the resignation of the entire Commission in March 1905, immediately naming a whole new Commission headed up by a three-man executive committee which was answerable only to Secretary Taft. Meanwhile, Wallace, who had again returned to Washington, decided to postpone his return to Panama by another month. It may have been that he was influenced by the news that the "sickly season" had arrived on the Isthmus, bringing with it yellow fever and malaria.

Although back in New York, Wallace was quoted as saying, "Everything is now proceeding in harmony, with a well-defined general plan," the truth was that morale in the Zone was at an all-time low. Hospitals had begun to fill up and local undertakers, wise in the ways of Panama, were stockpiling caskets at the railroad depot. One worker remembered the year 1905 vividly: "In front of the railroad station was a baggage coach marked with large letters *Funeral Car.* The one behind that was the *Hospital Car.* When we started down the road, we would pick up the dead ones and the sick would go in the *Hospital Car.*" During Wallace's absence, his twenty-nine-year-old chief architect died of yellow fever and was buried in one of Wallace's famous metal caskets.

Now both white and black workers were deserting the Isthmus as soon as they were able to book passage out, with three-quarters of the Americans having fled by the end of March 1905. *The New York Times* quoted a young worker's warning: "Tell the boys to stay at home if they get only a dollar a day." Newspapers and magazines were increasingly pessimistic. "Anyone of this generation might as well give up all hope of ever seeing the Canal completed," editorialized one, while another predicted a 1950 completion date. As for the black workers, a visiting writer reported, "I could not find a single man or woman who had not suffered or was not suffering from illness of some kind; not a single one of whom did not want to go home, but was prevented by want of money."

By the time Wallace and his wife returned to Panama in May 1905, the Zone was in the grip of panic. "Everybody here seems to be sitting on a tack," was how one employee described the tension. "The men at work shuddered as they passed the little French cemeteries so plentifully scattered along the Zone," wrote an observer.

Actually, with sixty-two cases of yellow fever and nineteen deaths, the yellow fever panic was far out of proportion to the danger, especially since pneumonia, tuberculosis, dysentery, typhoid fever, beri-beri and, above all, malaria had been taking a far higher toll for months, especially among black workers. Nevertheless, because no one took seriously his theory that mosquitoes carry both yellow fever and malaria, Dr. Gorgas, chief of the medical staff, was given absolutely no support or encouragement from either Wallace or the Commission.

Although Wallace had already been away from the Isthmus three out of the twelve months he had served as chief engineer, in June of 1905, only three weeks after returning to Panama, he and his wife again sailed for New York, supposedly to meet with Secretary Taft. Now word spread in the Zone that the unpopular Wallace was quitting, a rumor that plunged morale to a new low. Actually the rumors were only half-true. Upon meeting Taft in New York, Wallace announced that he had been offered another job for more money and although the offer was hard to refuse, he could be persuaded to stay on in Panama if he was made Commission chairman, given full control of all work and paid a higher salary. Wallace was playing a risky game.

Too risky. The usually good-humored Taft exploded. "You change your position overnight without thought to the embarrassing situation in which you place your government . . . you have thought of yourself and yourself alone," he stormed before demanding Wallace's immediate resignation.

Three days later, on June 28, 1905, President Roosevelt accepted Wallace's resignation at the same time that he released a complete transcript of the Taft–Wallace conversation. It goes without saying that the next day the newspapers were full of nothing else, with the resulting uproar not only damaging Roosevelt and his administration, but also the country's prestige around the world. In London the newspapers gloated that Roosevelt was now paying the price for his "land-piracy" in Panama. And back in Panama, a staff engineer summed up the workers' reaction bluntly: "We felt like an army deserted by its general." For all the criticism of the French, the American project, which had already wasted a year's time and cost millions of dollars, was in far worse shape than the French effort had ever been.

If Roosevelt's reputation was damaged by the resignation, Wallace's was damaged even more. A year later he told a Congressional committee that continuing under the Commission had been impossible. "I thought it better to sacrifice my ambitions regarding this work, which was to be the crowning event of my life, than remain to be humiliated, forced to disobey orders, or create friction." Although Wallace remained prominent in engineering circles for many years to come, he spent the rest of his life trying to justify his short term in the Zone as chief engineer . . . unsuccessfully.

Five

On the advice of Secretary of War Taft, President Roosevelt immediately appointed John Frank Stevens the new chief engineer. Like Wallace, the fifty-two-year-old Stevens was a railroad engineer, but unlike Wallace, he was a rugged wilderness man who had started as a track hand and worked his way up to building as many bridges, tunnels and railroads as any engineer in the world. Stevens's comment about Wallace perhaps said as much about Stevens as it did about Wallace: "Mr. Wallace was not an aggressive man, and there are times and conditions when fighting becomes a righteous duty."

When Stevens first met Roosevelt to discuss his new job, the president told him a story: "A certain man suddenly became wealthy and set up a large home. When his butler arrived he said to him, 'I don't know in the least what you are to do—but one thing I *do* know, you get busy and buttle like Hell!'"

Although that is just what Stevens was prepared to do, when he arrived in Panama on July 26, 1905, he realized that any kind of "buttling" simply wasn't possible. "I believe I faced about as discouraging a proposition as was ever presented to a construction engineer," he later wrote. "Nobody was working but the ants and the typists." There was no overall organization, while disease, not to mention fear of disease, had paralyzed the Isthmus so that Roosevelt's warning that "affairs are in a devil of a mess" was all too accurate. As to what the French had accomplished, Stevens dismissed it as merely "a big gash in the hills."

"There are three diseases in Panama," he announced. "They are yellow fever, malaria, and cold feet; and the greatest of these is cold feet." As his first order of business, Stevens stopped all excavation and began the kind of groundwork that Wallace should have tackled the year before. "The most important stage in any great undertaking is the preparatory stage," Stevens declared. "The digging is the least of all."

Appointed chief engineer in 1905, John Frank Stevens spends as little time as possible at his desk.

With a ninety percent turnover rate in the work force, Stevens knew that without workers the canal couldn't be built, and without decent, healthy living conditions, there wouldn't be any workers. Although chief medical officer Gorgas had received virtually no cooperation during the Wallace years, Stevens now promised him all the funds, supplies and manpower he needed to control disease. Next Stevens set to work building complete communities of houses, mess halls, barracks, hospitals, hotels, schools, churches and water and sewage systems.

By the end of 1906, half the canal employees were put to work constructing a total of 2,000 buildings. Stevens also organized clubs and baseball teams, ran weekly concerts and urged married men to send for their families. To encourage the single workers to marry, Stevens agreed to a plan devised by the head of housing, Jackson Smith (known as "Square-foot Smith"), whereby each employee was assigned one square foot of free housing for every dollar he earned, with wives receiving an additional square foot.

Recruiting offices were opened in the United States, Europe and the West Indies to hire workers, but despite the offer of an average monthly salary of $87, free housing and medical care, plus free transportation to Panama, only 3,243 Americans signed up for skilled jobs, 1,700 less than Stevens had hoped for. And of those who signed up, many weren't qualified. "I am not running a training school to teach boys engineering and construction," Stevens cabled back to Washington. "What I want is men who can go to work when they get here."

Although it was in violation of the 1903 treaty with Panama, Stevens and the Commission chairman decided to bypass the local Panamanian merchants by setting up department stores, or commissaries, that would sell food and supplies to workers at greatly reduced prices. He also arranged to have perishable foods such as eggs, vegetables, baked goods and ice delivered daily to the workers along the railroad line. Before long his efforts began to pay off. "Order has been brought out of the chaos, and system and discipline established," declared an American magazine writer after visiting the Isthmus.

Despite all his problems, Stevens was aware that the project had its advantages. Although the base of supplies was 2,000 miles away, unlike most engineering projects, there were no contracts to live up to, no property rights or outside traffic to worry about, an ample supply of unskilled labor and plenty of money to do the job. His first report to Washington included a typical Stevens remark: "There is no element of mystery . . . the problem is one of magnitude and not miracles."

To his credit, Stevens immediately realized, as the French and Wallace never had, that building the canal, especially at first, meant not only excavating the millions and millions of tons of dirt and rock that was called spoil but also removing it. "Efficient transportation is nearly always the key to success in construction," he explained. With that goal in mind, Stevens brought top railroadmen to the Isthmus and organized an efficient railroad system that would remove spoil quickly, as well as transport men, food and supplies wherever they were needed. "If dirt is to fly, there must be a smooth and uninterrupted movement of trains," he pointed out.

As to the Panama Railroad, Stevens described it as "two streaks of rust and a right of way." When an official pointed out

(Left) Stevens devises a railroad system that moves everything in the Canal Zone, including the work force.

that there had been no collisions on the main line, Stevens snapped back, "A collision has its good points as well as its bad ones, for it indicates that something is moving on the railroad."

Needless to say, conditions on the railroad didn't stay that way for long. In a year's time, Stevens had double-tracked the railroad so that it could go in both directions, laid heavier rails, reinforced bridges, updated signals and sidings, repaired or replaced worn-out equipment, installed a new telegraph and telephone system and ordered freight, dump, refrigerator cars and more than one hundred locomotives.

By early 1906, Stevens decided it was time to start excavating again. Like Wallace, he chose to use the mammoth American Bucyrus steam shovels for the heavy work. In comparison to the French shovels, Stevens said, they were "as an automobile to a baby carriage." And they needed to be. There was, after all, a staggering amount of earth to be excavated through the mountains of the Continental Divide. Nine miles of canal would eventually twist and turn through these mountains, a section known as Culebra Cut, Culebra meaning "snake" in Spanish and Cut being an engineering term for a man-made passageway or channel.

Day after day Stevens tramped along the line at Culebra Cut, talking to his men and checking every detail, all the while puffing away on such big cigars that he was soon affectionately known as "Big Smoke." A writer commented, "Chief Engineer Stevens is not an office engineer but a 'mixer.' You can never tell, the men say, when he will bob out from under some flat car." And it certainly wasn't long before he made his work methods known. "You may make mistakes," he cautioned, "but there is only one mistake you can make that will be fatal with me, and that is to do nothing."

Incredibly, even with the work progressing well, Congress still

Chief Engineer Stevens is never far from the work site.

hadn't decided whether to build a sea-level canal, which had been Wallace's choice, or a lock canal. Although an enormous amount of excavation had to be done either way, Stevens was understandably frustrated. "Give us the type of canal just as soon as you can. You must understand that I cannot, and I do not believe that any human being can do much more than mark time until that is done," he complained in a letter to Washington.

When Stevens had arrived in Panama, he had believed, like

The 1906 rainy season floods the Chagres River causing problems on the railroad.

almost everyone else, that the canal should be at sea level. But by November, he had witnessed the destructive rainy season, with its terrible flooding and the possibility of endless landslides and he realized that a sea-level canal would be such a "narrow, tortuous ditch" that ships would have to moor up endlessly to let other ships pass. He also estimated that a sea-level canal would not only take twice as long to build as a lock canal but also be much more expensive. By the time Stevens returned to Washington in December 1905, he had experienced such a complete turnaround, he was able to convince President Roosevelt, Secretary Taft and the Commission that a lock canal was the only workable choice.

Although Stevens hated to be away from his job (and also suffered from seasickness), he again sailed for Washington in January 1906, to urge the Senate Canal Committee to vote for a lock canal. In May an unhappy Stevens sailed for Washington to press his case a third time. In the end, he must have felt that all his trips to Washington were worth the effort, for in June 1906 both houses of Congress voted for a lock canal, probably the most momentous decision of the entire project.

The canal, which would cross one of the narrowest parts of the Isthmus, would run basically north and south, with the Pacific entrance twenty-seven miles farther east than the Atlantic en-

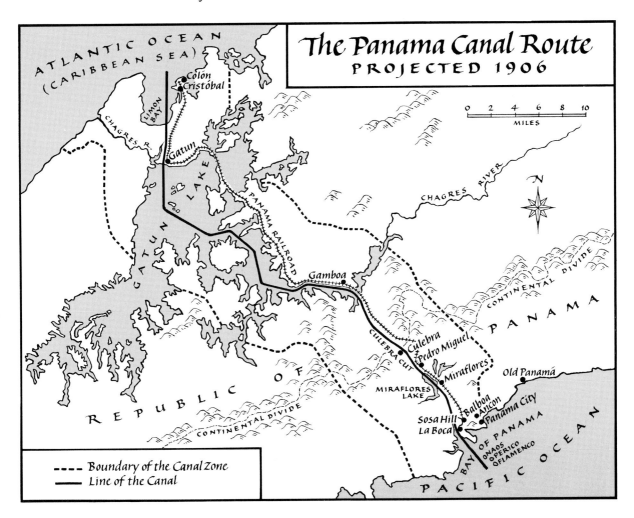

trance. A ship entering the canal from the Atlantic would follow a four-mile shipping channel from deep water across Limon Bay to the shoreline. From the Limon Bay shoreline, a three-mile sea-level channel would run inland to Gatun, where three locks would raise the ship eighty-five feet up to Gatun Lake. After traversing twenty-four miles across Gatun Lake, the ship would enter nine-mile-long Culebra Cut. At the southern end of Culebra Cut, a single lock at Pedro Miguel would lower the ship thirty feet down to Sosa Lake. At the far end of Sosa Lake, two more locks would lower the ship another fifty-five feet down to sea level at the Pacific entrance, where the ship would follow a four-mile channel across the Bay of Panama to deep water in the Pacific. All in all, it would be a fifty-mile voyage that would take about ten to twelve hours. Freshwater inland rivers would provide all the water in the canal, except for the sea-level channels at either end that would be supplied by salt water from the Atlantic and Pacific oceans.

In November 1906, President Theodore Roosevelt made his famous whirlwind trip to Panama to check progress on the canal. Upon his return to Washington, the president made a detailed report to Congress on everything he had seen, right down to the condition of the outhouses. "It is a stupendous work upon which our fellow countrymen are engaged in down there on the Isthmus," he said. With his three-day visit, Roosevelt had accomplished a great deal himself. He had ignited in the American people a sense that the country was united on a sacred crusade.

Back in the Zone, morale was high, with one employee admitting, "It was hell down here six months ago, but it's all right now." Work at Culebra Cut was proceeding so well, twice as much spoil was excavated in January 1907 as the French had excavated in their best month. With such excellent reports coming out of Panama, it can be imagined with what surprise President Roosevelt

(Right) Chief Engineer and Mrs. Stevens enjoy a Sunday afternoon ride.

received a letter from Stevens dated January 30, 1907, in which Stevens complained bitterly of the toll the job had taken on him and his family. He saw no glory in building the canal. "There has never been a day since my connection with this enterprise that I could not have gone back to the United States and occupied positions that to me, were far more satisfactory. Some of them, I would prefer to hold, if you will pardon my candor, than the Presidency of the United States."

Surprised or not, President Roosevelt decidedly did *not* pardon

Stevens's candor and he immediately cabled Stevens that his resignation, if that's what Stevens had meant it to be, was accepted.

The country was as shocked as the president. Some said that Stevens was unhappy over the canal plans, some said Mrs. Stevens had urged him to quit, others thought his health was poor, while still others claimed he had been offered a higher-paying job. Roosevelt, still stunned that Stevens didn't view the canal with the same religious zeal that he did, concluded, "If he were a drinking man or one addicted to the use of drugs, the answer would be simple. As it is, I am inclined to think that it must have been insomnia or something of the kind, due to his tropical surroundings."

"Surprise, disgust, and grief" was how an engineer on Stevens's staff described the reaction of the Zone work force. Although rumors flew, when Stevens was asked for his reasons, he merely replied, "Don't talk, dig." Even a petition urging him to stay, signed by 10,000 Zonians, couldn't change Big Smoke's mind.

In hindsight, it's likely that Stevens was exhausted and on the verge of a breakdown. He had written earlier, "I know that it is a very weak thing to say that a man is overworked, but I have had five hours' sleep in the last sixty." Whatever the cause, Stevens never revealed it. "The reasons for the resignation were purely personal. I have never declared these reasons and probably never will, as they are private," he later said. And he never did.

Resignation or not, Stevens's accomplishments on the canal were so significant that there are still those who believe he has never received proper credit. Even Roosevelt acknowledged to a friend, "He has done admirably." And it was certainly true that Stevens had been the right man on the canal at the right time. In his year and a half on the Isthmus, he had provided decent housing and food for his workers, organized a railroad system that was used throughout construction and drawn up plans for the work ahead. But of all his achievements, perhaps the most far-reaching had been his loyalty to, and support of, Dr. William Crawford Gorgas.

Chief Medical Officer Dr. William Gorgas finds a few moments of quiet on his porch.

Six

From his success in eliminating yellow fever in Havana three years before, Dr. Gorgas already knew that both yellow fever and malaria are carried by mosquitoes. The *Stegomyia fasciata* mosquito (now called the *Aëdes aegypti*) transmits yellow fever and the *Anopheles albimanus* mosquito transmits malaria. "The mosquito itself—there was the foe!" wrote Mrs. Gorgas. (Both she and Dr. Gorgas were immune to yellow fever after having survived earlier attacks.)

When the fifty-year-old Dr. Gorgas arrived on the Isthmus in 1904, he was aware that during the French years many more workers had died of malaria than yellow fever. But he was also aware that it was yellow fever that was terrorizing the Zone and yellow fever that he had to tackle first. Besides, yellow fever was his specialty. "We realized that the subject of yellow fever was by far the most important phase of sanitation with which we had to deal," he declared.

To transmit yellow fever, the female *Stegomyia* (the male is harmless) must suck the blood of a yellow fever patient that contains the yellow fever virus during the victim's first three days of illness. After twelve to twenty days, the infected *Stegomyia* can transmit the virus by biting another human. Because the female mosquito prefers human blood, she always deposits her 35 to 120 eggs in areas where there are people, and she will only deposit them in clean water such as can be found in containers or rain barrels. In less than ten days the mosquito larvae mature to adults in the water, with the adult having a life expectancy of about four weeks.

Because Gorgas and his staff had completely wiped out yellow fever in Havana in less than a year, he knew exactly what to do. First, he had to isolate all yellow fever victims to prevent any

Stegomyia from biting them and passing the virus on to others. Even more importantly, he had to eliminate the *Stegomyia* in the Zone. To do this, all standing fresh water had to be thrown out, covered or sprayed with a film of oil to prevent the female from laying her eggs in the water. Because larvae need air to breathe, the oil would also kill any larvae that were already in the water.

Gorgas was optimistic about success, especially since President Roosevelt had told the Commission that "the sanitary and hygienic problems . . . are those which are literally of the first importance, coming even before the engineering." But Gorgas was in for a surprise. Even though he had already proved that the *Stegomyia* causes yellow fever, no one paid any attention to his mosquito theory, the general opinion being that clean living and high ethical standards were protection enough. Although Chief Engineer Wallace was terrified of disease, he publicly announced that no "clean, healthy, moral American" was at risk from yellow fever.

Back in Washington, the Commission decided that eliminating mosquitoes was a ridiculous waste of time and money. "A dollar spent on sanitation is like throwing it into the bay," one Commissioner declared. When Gorgas arrived in Washington to plead for funds and supplies, the Commission told him, "On the mosquito you are simply wild. All who agree with you are wild. Get the idea out of your head."

Although Gorgas was the most good-natured of men, he was also stubborn and when he returned to Panama he was determined to pursue what he knew was the right course. Mrs. Gorgas later wrote about her husband, "That persistence which had always been his chief asset, however, still forced him to the task."

And then, in November of 1904, the first case of yellow fever was reported. With less than a fifty-fifty chance of survival once a

(Left) A portable cage isolates a yellow fever patient at Ancon Hospital.

person fell ill with yellow fever, there was nothing Gorgas or any other doctor could do but try to make the patient comfortable. The first symptoms were violent fits of shivering, high fever, a terrible thirst, severe headaches and vomiting. The symptoms eased in a few days but then the patient turned yellow, especially around the face and eyes. At this point the patient either survived (and was immune for life) or slipped into a fatal coma and died.

As more workers fell sick, "The Great Scare" took over. "Conditions in regard to yellow fever kept going from bad to worse in the first six months of 1905," Gorgas wrote. The Canal Zone governor agreed. "A feeling of alarm, almost amounting to panic, spread among the Americans on the Isthmus," he reported. Incredibly, the Commission still wasn't giving Gorgas the money, manpower or supplies that he needed. Furthermore, like other department heads, he was told to mail his orders rather than cabling them. The Commission even refused to ship two tons of newspaper that Gorgas needed to fumigate buildings on the mistaken belief that the newspapers were to be used for hospital reading material.

Gorgas had never been a quitter and fortunately he didn't quit now, for in July of 1905, John Stevens arrived in the Zone to replace Wallace as chief engineer. Gorgas and Stevens were both hardy frontiersmen who thrived on adversity and they became immediate friends. Although malaria, pneumonia, dysentery and tuberculosis were still taking more lives than yellow fever (and sickening two or three times the number who died), Stevens, like Gorgas, realized that it was *fear* of yellow fever that was paralyzing the Zone. He didn't believe the mosquito theory any more than Wallace had, but he knew that if he was ever going to keep workers on the Isthmus, he'd better back Gorgas all the way. And he did. Issuing an order that Gorgas's department was to get top priority, Stevens made sure that what Gorgas wanted, Gorgas got.

It was during this time that the Commission chairman, weary of Gorgas's constant demands for money and supplies, decided to replace him. But Stevens appealed to President Roosevelt to protest the decision and that was the end of that. Gorgas later wrote to Stevens, "You are the only one of the higher officials of the Isthmus who always supported the Sanitary Department. . . . So you can understand that our relations, yours and mine, stand out in my memory . . . as a green and pleasant oasis." Stevens, in turn, declared, "Colonel Gorgas was one of the finest characters I ever knew. His courage was an inspiration."

At last, with 4,000 workers assigned to him, Gorgas was able to start the most far-reaching and expensive sanitation program ever undertaken. While the Sanitation Department budget for 1904 had been $50,000, Gorgas now ordered $90,000 worth of copper screening alone (only copper could withstand Panama's humid climate), 50,000 gallons of kerosene and 200 barrels of larvacide a month, 3,000 garbage cans, 5,000 pounds of soap and 120 tons of insect powder, America's entire output for a year.

Two base hospitals had already been established, one at Colón on the Atlantic end of the canal and one at Ancon on the Pacific end. Hospital cars rode the railroad line twice a day picking up the sick and injured and delivering them to ambulances for transfer to one of the two base hospitals. "We transported a great many thousand patients this way without a mishap of any kind," Gorgas later bragged, and with 900 patients hospitalized on an average day, he deserved to brag.

Gorgas now divided the Zone into twenty-five districts, with an infirmary, an inspector, a doctor, a druggist and a cemetery in each. Meanwhile, all the towns in the Zone were supplied with running water which eliminated the need for water barrels and

A huge work force gets ready to fumigate all the buildings in Panama City.

containers. Next Gorgas had every room in every building throughout the Zone fumigated. After a building was evacuated and sealed tight with newspaper and paste, a small oven was filled with sulphur and lit. After the foul fumes had killed everything in the building, all the doors and windows were screened before the occupants were allowed back in.

Gorgas ordered kerosene to be sprayed on all standing water, with any container that might hold water destroyed, including the open pottery rings filled with water that had been placed around tree trunks on the Ancon Hospital grounds to discourage umbrella

(Right) Probably the most common sight in the Zone is a worker with a knapsack sprayer on his back oiling streams and pools.

ants and that had made the hospital a breeding ground for the *Stegomyia* for years.

Because the *Stegomyia*'s flight range is only 200 yards, brush and undergrowth were cleared within a 200-yard radius of all buildings. Every incoming ship was inspected and if there was yellow fever aboard, the ship was fumigated and any passengers or crew who couldn't prove they'd already had yellow fever were quarantined for six days in one of the Zone's two quarantine stations.

Much as Panamanians might have resented the Sanitary De-

partment's total dictatorship over their lives, not to mention the indignity of having their homes fumigated, by terms of the 1903 treaty they had no choice. A person could even be fined for tossing away a tin can. An observer pointed out, "We can send in a regiment if necessary to compel a man to keep his yard clean."

And then in 1906, the battle against yellow fever was won. Gorgas wrote, "By November the last case of this disease had occurred in Panama." At an autopsy of a yellow fever victim, he told his staff, "Take a good look at this man, boys, for it's the last case of yellow fever you will ever see." And it was.

Even before he'd eliminated yellow fever, Gorgas had mapped out his attack on malaria. Typically, malaria, which can recur for the rest of a person's life, begins six to twelve days after the victim has been bitten by an *Anopheles* mosquito that is carrying the malaria parasite. Chills, uncontrollable shivering and chattering teeth that last for about fifteen minutes are followed by about eight hours of high fever, burning thirst and a rapid pulse. When the fever breaks, the patient is drenched with sweat. The attacks tend to recur every three days, with recovery taking several weeks. Those who live through an attack feel wrung out mentally and physically, often to the point of serious depression, like the Chinese workers who had committed suicide after surviving malaria during the railroad-building years.

Gorgas already knew that just as only the female *Stegomyia* can transmit the yellow fever virus, only the female *Anopheles* mosquito can transmit the malaria parasite, the difference being that the *Anopheles* deposits her eggs not just in clean water but in water that collects anywhere, in a stagnant swamp, a clogged drain, a broken dish, even in the muddy hoof print of an animal. Because Gorgas didn't know much more than that, he had workers collect *Anopheles* larvae and pupae all along the canal route for

(Right) Oil to be sprayed on high grass and brush is heated so that it will run more smoothly.

study. To his alarm, Gorgas soon learned that the *Anopheles* is a "country" mosquito, with a longer flight range than the *Stegomyia,* that thrives literally anywhere except in sunny, open areas. With a life span of about a month, the infected female feeds on blood approximately once every two or three nights, which means she is capable of transmitting the malaria parasite at least ten to fifteen times.

One of Gorgas's assistants counted 54 *Anopheles* mosquitoes on a single hospital doorway and when Gorgas examined 500 West Indians living in a Zone village, he discovered that every one of them showed symptoms of active malaria or of past attacks. Because the *Anopheles* bite can't always be felt, after only a month or so of research, almost the entire medical staff, including Gorgas, had come down with malaria.

Knowing that the *Anopheles* mosquito needs grass or algae as

Drainage ditches are lined with concrete and mopped with oil to prevent mosquitoes from breeding. Housing for the West Indian workers is seldom supplied with screens.

protection from sunshine and wind, Gorgas sent out squads of workers to cut down or burn high grass and sheltering brush. Garbage was buried and hundreds of miles of drainage ditches were dug and lined with concrete so that grass couldn't grow. Oil or larvacide, which was a mixture of carbolic acid, resin and alkali, was sprayed on pools, streams and swamps. A certain kind of minnow that thrives on mosquito larvae was imported, bred and released into streams and lakes.

In an attempt to persuade the workers to take quinine every day to prevent their blood from harboring the malaria parasite, Gorgas had quinine tonic and quinine pills available in every dining hall. A former West Indian worker recalled the bitter "Panama

Cocktail": "Every morning they come through and give you a dose of quinine. If you drink it it's all right, but some of us hold it in our mouth . . . but if he see you, you get double dose."

Certainly Gorgas's all-out attack helped reduce the number of malaria cases, especially in populated areas where eliminating the *Stegomyia* had also eliminated a certain number of *Anopheles*. But because dense jungle and swamp were never far away, it was impossible to destroy all *Anopheles* breeding places, so that malaria continued to take a higher toll than all other diseases combined. A West Indian worker reminisced, "Well, the saddest experience I have seen, that I have ever had, men walk down and drop dead with malaria. . . . You walk together today and the man would drop dead, malaria." Gorgas himself said in 1915, "I was much disappointed that we did not get rid of malaria on the Isthmus of Panama."

Nevertheless, records show that in 1906 there were 821 malaria cases for every 1,000 Zonians, while by 1913 there were only 76 for every 1,000. In his report to Congress after returning from Panama in 1906, President Roosevelt praised Gorgas's work: "The results have been astounding . . . just at present the health on the Isthmus is remarkably good." Typically modest, Gorgas gave much of the credit to Stevens: ". . . it is hard to estimate how much sanitation on the Isthmus owes to this gentleman."

Without Gorgas's efforts, Stevens pointed out, "another dismal failure would have been recorded and we would have had no Panama Canal today." He was probably right. As a fine doctor who tolerated criticism with patience, a researcher who stood by his convictions, the only staff member to serve on the Isthmus from the beginning years to the end, Dr. William Crawford Gorgas remains one of the true heroes of the Panama Canal.

Seven

What an uproar followed the announcement that Chief Engineer Stevens had resigned! "Today the whispers, winks and chuckles were much in evidence. The anti-Roosevelt Senate crowd . . . will probe for mud with which to plaster the President and Taft," reported *The New York Times.*

It wasn't as if President Roosevelt didn't already know that both he and the canal were in trouble. After all, it was less than three years into the work and two chief engineers had already quit. This time, Roosevelt declared, he would put the canal "in charge of men who will stay on the job till I get tired of having them there, or till I say they may abandon it. I shall turn it over to the army."

Which is just what he did. On February 26, 1907, President Roosevelt announced the appointment of forty-eight-year-old Lieutenant Colonel George Washington Goethals as chief engineer. In response to his new assignment, former West Pointer

In 1907 President Roosevelt names Colonel George W. Goethals to be chief engineer, at the same time detaching him from the army.

Goethals wrote to a friend, "It's a case of just plain straight duty. I am ordered down—there was no alternative."

Back on the Isthmus everyone was unhappy that the army was about to take over and that an army colonel was to be chief engineer. Actually, because President Roosevelt had detached Goethals and the other newly-appointed army engineers from the military, the Army Corps of Engineers had nothing whatsoever to do with building the canal. Furthermore, Goethals had never fought in a war or even fired a gun except on the practice range.

"I am no longer a commander in the United States Army," he announced at his official, not-very-cordial reception in Panama City in March 1907. "I now consider that I am commanding the Army of Panama, and that the enemy we are going to combat is the Culebra Cut and the locks and dams at both ends of the Canal."

To his surprise, Goethals was impressed indeed by what he found on his arrival in the Zone, especially when he compared it to what he had seen during an earlier visit with Secretary Taft soon after Stevens had taken over as chief engineer. (At the time Stevens, who had no great fondness for Goethals, had rejected Taft's suggestion that Goethals serve as his assistant.) Goethals's generous comment about Stevens revealed more about the speaker than it did about his subject: "We are building on the foundations he (Stevens) laid, and the world cannot give him too much credit."

Never a modest man, Stevens had an equally high opinion of his efforts. "You don't need me any longer," he had told his work force before sailing for home. "All you have to do now is to dig a ditch. What you want is a statesman."

But the work ahead demanded far more than a statesman. Although preparations were well underway, surveys hadn't been completed, the Panama Railroad had to be relocated for the creation of Gatun Lake, harbor improvements were needed, the work in Culebra Cut was barely begun and the complicated system of locks, dams, spillways and powerhouses hadn't even been designed.

Throughout his year and a half on the Isthmus, one of Stevens's strongest assets had been his relationship with his workers.

At his farewell party, a speaker said, "While Mr. Stevens has not been an easy taskmaster, he won the respect and even the love of all his employees." On the day Big Smoke left the Isthmus, thousands of emotional workers arrived at the dock by special trains to present him with a gold watch, a diamond ring, a silver tea service and two bound volumes filled with ten thousand signatures.

Unlike Stevens, the rather stiff-necked Goethals tended to be ill at ease with people and was so unpopular at first that a number of his staff resigned. Perhaps the chief engineers' respective nicknames were an indication of how workers regarded the two men: Stevens's "Big Smoke" in contrast to Goethals's "The Colonel." An engineer on Goethals's staff later wrote, "I was his assistant for seven years, and I might say that everything in my life since has seemed comparatively easy."

Other staff members kept their distance, too, especially Dr. Gorgas whose relationship with Goethals was always cool, especially after Goethals, in an effort to save money, took all responsibility for brush-clearing and grass-cutting away from Gorgas's department. Gorgas later claimed that decision was one of the main reasons he had never totally been able to eliminate malaria in the Zone. Mrs. Gorgas, who described Goethals as humorless and dictatorial, related an encounter between the two men.

"Do you know, Gorgas, that every mosquito you kill costs the United States Government ten dollars?" Goethals asked.

"But just think," Gorgas replied, "one of those ten-dollar mosquitoes might bite you, and what a loss that would be to the country."

There was no question that Goethals set incredibly high standards for his staff but it was also true that he demanded far more from himself than from anyone else, usually working a twelve- or fourteen-hour day, with almost no time off. As the months passed and as Goethals's judgment, basic fairness and obvious abilities became apparent, opinion began to shift. "It is plain to me that the work is well in hand, and that the Colonel is becoming daily more the master of the situation," wrote Goethals's secretary, Joseph Bishop, to President Roosevelt in August 1907, adding, "He goes to the spot, sees what is needed, gives a plain direct order and gets results instead of excuses." A pleased Roosevelt replied to Bishop, "Goethals is exactly the man for the work. How fortunate we have been to get him!"

Bishop, who was also secretary of the Commission, had been assigned to Goethals to report back to Roosevelt everything that was happening in the Zone, especially any problem that might be hindering progress. Now, at Bishop's suggestion, Goethals began a weekly newspaper, the *Canal Record*, which was filled with information and news concerning work on the canal, prices of food, social events, ship sailings, obituaries or anything else that might be of interest to Zonians.

At Bishop's suggestion, Goethals began holding open house every Sunday morning to hear problems or complaints from any Commission employee or dependent. With the work force numbering 32,000 by the end of 1907, Goethals met with approximately 100 people each Sunday, a labor practice well ahead of its time. It was these sessions more than anything else that boosted Goethals in the workers' esteem. "They were treated like human beings, not like brutes and they responded by giving the best service within their power," Bishop wrote to the president.

In response to all the positive news from the Isthmus, in January 1908, Roosevelt named Goethals to be Commission chairman, answerable only to the president through Secretary of War Taft. Although the 1902 Spooner Act stated that the chief engineer was to be under the direction of the Commission, Goethals later commented that the president took the opportunity "to assume powers which the law did not give him but which it did not forbid him to exercise."

Now, as chairman of the Commission, chief engineer and head of the Panama Railroad, too, Goethals became absolute Czar of the Zone. Writer Willis Abbot commented, "No President of the United States, not even Lincoln in war times, exerted the au-

President Roosevelt appoints Goethals chairman of the Isthmian Canal Commission in 1908. Left to right: Jackson Smith, Joseph Bucklin Bishop, Dr. William Gorgas, Rear Admiral Harry Rousseau, Colonel Goethals, Major David Gaillard, Senator Joseph Blackburn, Major William Sibert.

thority he daily employed in the zenith of his power.'' Goethals was now able to overrule any decision concerning the canal, housing, schools, the police, fire department or the courts. All magazine articles about the Canal Zone had to be submitted to Goethals for his approval . . . or rejection. He had the authority to hire, deport, transfer, fire or evict workers or their dependents for any reason.

During one of Goethals's Sunday sessions, a Jamaican woman complained that her out-of-work husband kept all her earnings. When Goethals ordered the man to return the money, the man pointed out that under English law a husband could keep his wife's wages.

"All right," the Colonel is reported to have said. "You're from Jamaica. I'll deport you both and you can get all the English law you want."

(The husband promptly returned the money.)

And Goethals seemed to be everywhere at once. He daily inspected the line of work in his private railroad car, which had been dubbed the "Yellow Peril." Painted a bright yellow, the car, said Bishop, looked like "the nightmare offspring of a passenger engine and a taxi." But its appearance was no joke. Bishop continued, "You could scare a shirker out of a wet season's growth by yelling, 'Here comes the Yellow Peril!'"

As to the actual work, Goethals reorganized the Canal Zone into three sections, the Atlantic Division, the Central Division and the Pacific Division, with a head engineer to be in charge of each division. Now the time had come. Goethals was ready for full-scale war against the geological forces of the Zone and for his first battle, he chose Culebra Cut, that nine-mile section of the Central Division that had to be excavated through the mountains of the Continental Divide . . . and was referred to by some as Hell's Gorge.

(Left) Goethals and his Washington visitors prepare to tour the canal route in the Yellow Peril.

Eight

"This is the most formidable part of the enterprise," Goethals said, referring to the channel that had to be dug through the mountains of the Continental Divide. Difficult as he knew the job was going to be, Goethals had the foresight, and the courage, to widen Culebra Cut from 200 to 300 feet even though the decision meant half again as much spoil would have to be removed at an additional cost of $14 million.

Because transiting ships would pass directly between Culebra Cut and Gatun Lake, the water in both had to be the same level. Since Gatun Lake was going to be eighty-five feet above sea level, the water in Culebra Cut, or the Cut, as it was called, would have to be eighty-five feet above sea level, too. For ships to travel in the Cut, the water needed to be forty-five feet deep, which meant that the entire length of the Cut would have to be taken down to a depth of forty feet above sea level. The section that would require the most excavation would be the 312-foot-above-sea-level ridge that stretched between Gold Hill and Contractors Hill, the two highest mountains in the Cut.

To complicate the job, the Cut's torrential rains and suffocating heat resulted in almost unbearable working conditions. By noon the temperature at the bottom of the Cut was around 100 degrees, at times rising to 120 or even 130. A West Indian worker remembered the Cut only too well: "There was no shelter from the sun or the rain, see. There was no trees. . . . And when the sun shine, you get it. When the rain falls, you get it. When the wind blows, you get it."

Because an enormous amount of blasting was necessary, Major David Gaillard, head of the Central Division, which included both Gatun Lake and Culebra Cut, put half his work force, about 3,000 men, on dynamite detail. With some fifteen million pounds of dynamite and blasting powder shipped to the Isthmus in the year 1910 alone, workers were needed all along the route, from the initial unloading of the ships in the harbor to the final delivery of the dynamite to the drillers.

Skilled drillers used either a well drill or a tripod drill, both of which were powered by compressed air, to drill holes for the dynamite. With more than 300 drills going at once, the racket was deafening, especially when the drills had to bite through solid

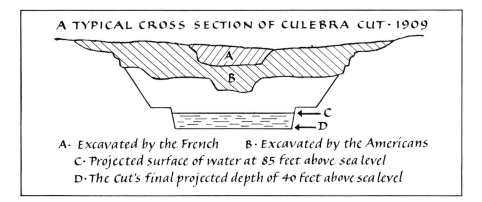

A TYPICAL CROSS SECTION OF CULEBRA CUT · 1909

A· Excavated by the French   B· Excavated by the Americans
C· Projected surface of water at 85 feet above sea level
D· The Cut's final projected depth of 40 feet above sea level

West Indian workers in Culebra Cut load and tamp dynamite into deep holes drilled earlier.

rock. Although the holes were anywhere from fifteen to twenty-seven feet deep, they were so narrow that small charges had to be detonated to enlarge the holes at the bottom for the main charges. Once the 75- to 200-pound main charges were loaded in the holes, they were tamped in place and the fuses set. For obvious reasons, the charges weren't detonated until the workers had left the Cut, either at lunch time or after five o'clock. The *Canal Record* reported, "The blasting goes on without end."

Despite all sorts of precautions, the threat of accidents always hung over the Cut. Premature explosions, steam shovels striking unexploded charges, lightning hitting a charge and above all, human error, took a terrible toll. The worst disaster of the construction years occurred on December 12, 1908, when 44,000 pounds of dynamite that had been loaded in 52 holes went off accidentally, killing 26 workers and injuring more than 40. "That you see bits of men here and a head yonder. Oh, they were picking it up for days. Oh, boy! That wasn't an easy day, I tell you. Sunday morning," recalled a West Indian worker.

Once the charges had been detonated, the spoil was loaded onto dirt trains by steam shovels, the same dependable Bucyrus steam shovels that both Wallace and Stevens had used. The largest of the steam shovels could pick up five cubic yards (approximately eight tons) in its dipper as it excavated a fifty-foot-wide by twelve-foot-deep swath. If the rocks were too big for the shovels to handle, they were broken up by "dobie" blasting, that is, three or more sticks of dynamite were placed on the rock, covered with mud and lit with a slow fuse. The steam shovels, which were fueled by coal and ran on tracks like a locomotive, were operated by ten-man crews. So as not to slow down work during the day, coal trains came into the Cut at night to refuel the shovels. Repair gangs, too, overhauled and repaired the machines at night.

With the *Canal Record* publishing weekly excavation statistics for every steam shovel, production levels, as well as rivalry, skyrocketed. "We were going along doing what we thought was a fair day's work . . . (then) away we went like a pack of idiots trying to get records for ourselves," commented one shovel operator. From 1907 on, an average of thirty-seven steam shovels were in the Cut at all times, with each shovel excavating something over a million cubic yards a year. A record was set in March 1909, when more than four million cubic yards of spoil were removed by sixty-eight shovels, the greatest number of shovels that ever operated at one time.

"Culebra Cut was primarily a transportation problem," Stevens had said, and certainly removing the millions of tons of spoil that the dynamite and shovels excavated was at the heart of the operation. The railroad system Stevens had devised that daily carried the spoil out of the Cut in 200 dirt trains was so efficient, Goethals depended on it throughout the construction years.

Each dirt train was made up of one-sided flat cars connected to each other by a steel sheet that made the twenty cars into one continuous unit. In order for the long arms of the shovels to dump the spoil directly into the dirt cars, the shovels worked on terraces along the side of the mountain, with the dirt trains on terraces directly above them. Because the shovels started at either end of the Cut and advanced toward the middle, or summit of the mountains, they worked on the upgrade with their noses into the bank. As the excavation went deeper, the steam shovels worked on lower and lower terraces, which meant that both the shovel tracks and the dirt-train tracks had to be lowered, too.

Once the dirt trains were loaded with the Cut's colorful spoil of black dirt, red clay and yellow, brown and blue rock, they rolled out of the Cut on the downgrade at the same time that empty cars were returning by another track on the upgrade. Yardmasters stationed in towers at either end of the Cut directed each train to one of sixty dumping grounds located outside of the Cut. Some of the spoil was used to fill in swampland, some was used to construct earthen dikes, dams and embankments, while a lot of it was simply disposed of.

The dumps, which covered as much as a thousand acres, were a network of railroad tracks on different levels, with each incoming dirt train assigned to a particular track. Once the train was on the proper track, a huge steel plow was hauled from one end of the train to the other, unloading the spoil from all twenty cars at once, a job that would have taken hundreds of men to do by hand. A railroad car mounted with enormous steel plows then pushed the spoil down the embankment. Because the dump's railroad tracks often slid out of place in the mud, a track shifter was designed that could lift and move whole sections of track up to nine feet in any direction, another saving of countless man-hours.

Joseph Bishop described Culebra Cut as "a swarming mass of men and rushing railway trains, monster-like machines all working with ceaseless activity, without confusion or conflict anywhere." And it was true. In order that one operation not interfere with any other, the location of every steam shovel, section of track and work crew was carefully plotted out each day under the direction of Major Gaillard on a huge map at Central Division headquarters.

Although work in the Cut was highly organized, it looked like chaos. In 1911 an employee noted, "Everywhere there are gangs of men . . . shovel gangs, track gangs, surfacing gangs, dynamite gangs, gangs doing everything imaginable with shovel and pick and crowbar, gangs down on the floor of the canal, gangs far up the steep walls of cut rock, gangs stretching away in every direction." The noise from the Cut was chaotic, too. "The sounds were harsh, deafening, brutal, such as we might fancy would arise from hell were the lid of that place of fire and torment to be lifted," wrote observer Willis Abbot in 1912.

One problem that neither Gaillard nor anyone else could organize was the amount of water that continuously flooded the Cut, both from the torrential rains of the wet season and the many small streams and rivers that crisscrossed the Cut or drained into it. With the average rainfall in the Cut about 79 inches a year,

1909 set a record on the Isthmus, with one town in the Zone reporting 237 inches of rain (as compared to 50 inches in Washington D.C. for the same year).

To keep the Cut as free of water as possible, Gaillard installed drains and pumps, built dikes and had diversion channels dug that would carry water out of the Cut. But water still seeped up

through the ground or freshets poured into the Cut, flooding tracks, submerging shovels and halting all work, sometimes for days at a time. Goethals described the water in the Cut as "an ever-existing problem."

Furthermore, the heavy rains of the wet season turned the top layer of loose dirt, sand, gravel and stone into a pudding-like mud that flowed down the slopes of the Cut like a slow-motion avalanche. Although Wallace and Stevens had dealt with mud slides in a minor way, almost as soon as Goethals took over as chief engineer, there was a major mud slide in the area known as Cucaracha (Spanish for "cockroach"). In 1907 fifty acres of mud and rock slid down the slopes into the Cut at a rate of ten to fifteen feet a day, burying steam shovels, twisting railroad tracks and moving whole trains hundreds of feet. "It was, in fact, a tropical glacier—of mud instead of ice," was how Gaillard described

(Left) With flooding a constant problem in Culebra Cut, a gang of men is put to work digging a diversion ditch by hand. (Above) Two coal-powered steam shovels that run on tracks clear out a mud slide at Cucaracha.

the slide that took over a month to clear out. And that was only the beginning. From then on, Cucaracha moved almost continuously, with two major slides in 1910 that bottlenecked the Cut for months.

As more of the mountains were excavated and the Cut grew wider, the slides became more serious. In one area the earth slid so slightly no real damage was done, although work gangs did nothing for two years but move railroad tracks back where they belonged. Gaillard announced optimistically in 1911 that "the greatest trouble with slides has already been experienced." But he was wrong. That same year it took three months to remove the mud in the Cut and more than four months in 1912. Just before the Cut was finished in 1913, another slide at Cucaracha flowed down the slopes, crossed the Cut and went sixty-seven feet up the other side. Goethals's reaction when asked what he was going to do now? "Hell," he replied, "dig it out again." And they did.

Much to everyone's surprise, as excavation continued, another kind of slide developed that had nothing to do with the rainy season and was even more destructive than the mud slides. Caused by unstable rock, the height of the slopes and the side effects of heavy blasting, so-called dry slides began as huge cracks along the rim of the Cut. As the channel through the Cut deepened and the angle of the slope became steeper, the underlying rock couldn't withstand the enormous weight from above, causing the exposed wall of the Cut simply to buckle outward and crack. Once the big sections of earth, often acres in size, gave way at the crack, they slid slowly down the slope taking everything with them.

As the slides moved downward, their tremendous weight forced the earth upward at the point of least resistance, which in this case was the floor of the Cut. Sometimes the floor would silently rise ten, fifteen or even twenty feet. Gaillard was once

(Right) Steam Shovel #258 and the dirt train next to it are thrown off their tracks by yet another slide, May 1913.

astonished to see a steam shovel sinking before his eyes until he realized that the shovel wasn't sinking, the ground where he stood was rising, about six feet in five minutes! The weird heaving-up of the Cut floor, combined with clouds of steam created by the friction of huge masses of stone and gravel acting on ground water, convinced many a reporter, not to mention worker, that active volcanoes were about to erupt.

The worst of the dry slides was in 1910 when huge cracks appeared in front of the town of Culebra high on the rim of the Cut. A young Zone wife said, ''Now suddenly the people living nearest the Cut were being compelled to move: the bank was slid-

ing into the Cut!'' Two rows of cottages, Division headquarters, a prison stockade and the Zone's largest YMCA clubhouse had to be torn down and rebuilt elsewhere. Moving at a rate of about three feet a day, seventy-five acres of the town eventually broke away and slid into the Cut.

In desperation, Gaillard even tried using concrete to hold back the slides, but all that happened was that the concrete broke up and slid into the Cut along with everything else. ''The chief geologist declared that they (the slides) would not cease until the angle of the Canal bank became so gentle that gravity would not pull the crest down,'' Willis Abbot explained. Although the solution sounded simple, it meant that the banks had to be cut back and back to lessen the angle of the slopes. The distance at the top between one side of the Cut and the other side had originally been 840 feet, but by the time the Cut was finished, the distance measured almost 2,000 feet.

In the end, Culebra Cut came close to winning the battle. A West Indian worker said later, "I personally say to my fellow men, that my children would come and have children, and their children would come and do the same, before you would see water in the Cut." Another worker commented, "Culebra gave the Americans quite a boxing match." Before the job was finished, almost one-quarter of all the spoil that was taken out of the Cut was a result of the twenty-six slides that moved hundreds of acres into the Cut.

With all the publicity, Culebra Cut became a major tourist attraction. In the beginning, tourists by the hundreds arrived by

(Left) Work terraces are still in evidence as Culebra Cut at last begins to resemble a canal. (Above) With water released into the Cut, tourists gather to watch dredges finish up the excavation.

special trains from Colón and Panama City but as the excavation went deeper and the slides became more dramatic, they came by the thousands, 9,800 in 1911 and nearly 15,000 in 1912. Standing on the rim hundreds of feet above the incredible noise and smoke of the Cut, the tourists might well have agreed with a reporter who declared, "He who did not see Culebra Cut during the mighty work of excavation missed one of the great spectacles of the ages."

At last, on May 20, 1913, Steam Shovel #222 and Steam Shovel #230, advancing from opposite directions, met on the bottom of the canal in an historic moment. A shovel operator's wife recalled the scene: "We looked down at the men shaking hands and clapping each other on the back and could see the two shovels

Every steam whistle in the Cut blasts in celebration as Steam Shovels #222 and #230 working from opposite directions meet on May 20, 1913.

The momentous meeting of the two steam shovels is photographed from either end.

with their booms raised and dippers almost touching . . . the last barrier was down." The full nine-mile length of Culebra Cut was forty feet above sea level from end to end. "The way that they brought down that high mountain up there and bring it all the way down to the bottom. They break the back of the Isthmus, you see," marveled a former worker.

And indeed they had.

Nine

"The one great problem in the construction of any canal down there is the control of the Chagres River. That overshadows everything else," Chief Engineer John Stevens had told a Senate Committee in 1906 when he was urging them to vote for a lock canal. Not only would the 120-mile river cross the route of a sea-level canal 22 times on its journey from Panama's heartland to the Atlantic Ocean, but it had also been known to rise more than 25 feet in a single day, flooding everything in its path.

When Colonel Goethals took over as chief engineer, he agreed with Stevens, saying, "The greatest difficulty of the Panama route is the control of the Chagres River." Actually, the lock-canal plan that the Americans settled on was almost identical to a plan that de Lesseps had rejected in 1879. It called for an earthen dam across the Chagres River three miles inland from the Atlantic Ocean near Gatun village. The dam would serve two purposes: it would control the raging river and it would create a huge lake that would provide most of the fresh water needed to operate the canal. The

Gatun location was chosen because the Chagres River flowed through a valley that was only a mile and a half wide at that point and was bounded on either side by low rocky hills to which an earthen dam could be connected. When the dam was finished, it would extend the full mile and a half across the valley and cover almost 300 acres, making it the largest earthen dam in the world.

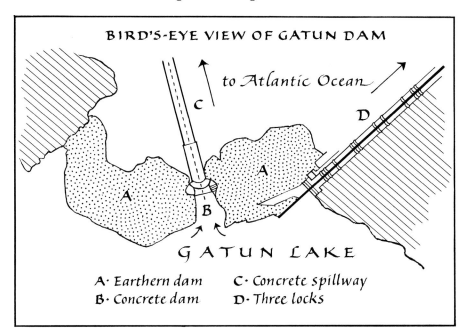

BIRD'S-EYE VIEW OF GATUN DAM

to Atlantic Ocean

C

D

A

A

B

GATUN LAKE

A· Earthern dam   C· Concrete spillway
B· Concrete dam   D· Three locks

In the middle of the valley was a small rocky hill on which a concrete dam and spillway was to be constructed. The concrete dam, set in the center of the earthen dam, would control the level of Gatun Lake by releasing water from the lake when the water level of the lake was too high or by retaining water in the lake when the water level was too low. Because Gatun Lake would be eighty-five feet above sea level and the channel that led to it from the Atlantic Ocean would be at sea level, three sets of locks built next to the dam would be needed to raise or lower ships from one level to another. The sea-level channel, Gatun Dam and the three sets of locks made up the Atlantic Division.

Construction of the earthen dam called for two parallel rock walls across the entire mile-and-a-half width of the valley. These rock walls, which were called "toes" or retaining walls, would be approximately a quarter of a mile apart. A mixture of sand, clay and mud that was the consistency of thick soup and called "fill," would be pumped in between the walls. Over time, the heavier materials would settle to the bottom, while the water and the lighter particles would be carried away through drain pipes. Once these materials began to harden, dry spoil, mostly from Culebra Cut, would be dumped on top of them. The weight of the spoil would squeeze out the last bit of moisture so that the material between the two parallel retaining walls that would form the dam itself would eventually be as solid as concrete.

When the dam plans were made public, there were immediate objections. Gatun's porous rock and unstable mud wouldn't support such an enormous dam; the dam's foundations were inadequate; the dam wouldn't be watertight; an earthen dam could never withstand the pressure from a 164-square-mile body of water that was to be the world's largest man-made lake. "Around no other structure in the history of engineering did the fires of controversy rage so furiously and persistently as they raged for several years around Gatun Dam," Willis Abbot wrote.

It wasn't as if Goethals weren't already coping with enough technical problems. The waters of Gatun Lake would eventually flood almost all the excavation work the French had completed, as well as miles of the newly repaired Panama Railroad, many of the communities Stevens had built, a dozen native villages and thousands of acres of jungle.

Nevertheless, shortly after Goethals arrived on the Isthmus in

1907, he gave the order for Major William Sibert, head of the Atlantic Division, to begin construction on the dam. Sibert, whose personality was very much like John Stevens's, right down to the ever-present black cigar and somewhat chilly relationship with Goethals, divided the work on the mile-and-a-half-long dam into three parts: the eastern section, the western section and the concrete dam and spillway that made up the middle section.

To be on the safe side, Sibert had a scale model built of the dam and adjoining three locks in a watertight tank to make certain that they would hold up under the pressure of the water. He also ordered the drilling of hundreds of test pits and borings to be sure that the subsurface would support the weight of construction. Despite the announcement that both Sibert and Goethals were satisfied with the results, criticism of the plans became so vocal that President Roosevelt finally had to step in and send Secretary Taft, three engineers and two Congressmen to Panama to check out the situation.

"A special committee of engineers individually entered each of the test pits, the deepest of which was extended to a depth of 87.4 feet and disproved the rumor," came back the report. Even the

300-pound Taft had been lowered (reluctantly) into a pit by a canal staff engineer who later said, "I was mighty glad to get him out of there. He was a big man and the rope on the windlass looked awfully small."

With the uproar stilled, at least temporarily, Sibert began construction of the eastern

Secretary of War Taft [left] is sent to Panama to consult with Goethals and inspect the Gatun Dam site.

section of the dam. In order to keep the work area dry, he filled in the Chagres River channels in the eastern section and widened and deepened the channels in the western section so that they could handle the full flow of the river. Next he had railway trestles built directly above where the two retaining walls for the eastern section would eventually rise. From these trestles, railroad cars dumped tons and tons of broken rock to build up the walls. When the high wooden trestles themselves became embedded in rock, Sibert laid the railroad tracks on top of the walls. As the rock walls grew higher and higher, he had the railroad tracks moved up on terraces.

Sibert already knew that the increasing weight of the rock walls would cause them to sink in the mud, silt and clay of the subsoil as they settled down to solid bedrock. In the process of settling, the surface of the rock walls often shifted and sank, sometimes throwing the railroad tracks out of line or even sliding trains off their tracks. Although the constant shifting meant that train gangs had to keep moving the tracks back where they belonged, it was nothing more than what Sibert had expected.

Not so the public. On November 21, 1908, a reporter who wandered over to Gatun Dam in search of a story found a big one, or at least thought he had. During the night a portion of rock wall had sunk twenty feet, causing the Chagres River to flood the railroad tracks on top of it. Because the reporter didn't realize that this happened all the time, he wrote a sensational account of how Gatun Dam was being built on an underground lake. Newspapers all over the world picked up the story. COLLAPSE OF GATUN DAM, one headline blazoned, while another bannered, GATUN DAM IS SAID TO HAVE SUNK 60 FEET. A French newspaper gloated, PREDICT FAILURE AT PANAMA.

Goethals, who hadn't even been told about the minor shifting

(Right) A staff member examines the slippage on Gatun Dam's rock retaining wall, November 21, 1908.

of track, was caught off guard. At this point, talk about the dam collapsing was ridiculous. Work had only begun on the retaining walls of the eastern section, nothing had been done on the western section through which the Chagres River still flowed and not one cubic yard of fill had been pumped to form the dam itself. It was the same old story: no one back in the United States had any idea it would take thousands of men and the largest, most modern construction machinery in the world five years just to complete rough work on the dam. Even the *Canal Record* explained that "the work on the dam is not in any way interrupted by these small settlings." But because the Battle of the Levels was still raging back in the United States, sea-level advocates seized the opportunity to argue that the collapse of Gatun Dam proved that a lock canal could never work.

In January 1909, an annoyed President Roosevelt had to organize another panel of engineers, again headed by William Howard Taft, who had just been elected president but had not yet taken

office, to travel to Panama. Reassuring Roosevelt ''as to the safe, tight, and durable quality of Gatun Dam,'' the engineers found the work was going so well, they recommended that the dam be lowered from a height of 135 feet to 115 feet (later to 105 feet). ''It is not necessary to tie a horse with a log chain to make sure he can not break away. A smaller chain would serve just as well,'' reported one of the experts.

After two unnecessary trips to Panama, Taft was tired of all the rumors, too. ''There is nothing so discouraging as a fire in the rear,'' he told an audience shortly after his return to the United States. ''That kind of fire in the rear is calculated to break down the nervous system of those persons on the Isthmus working day and night, tooth and toenail to build the greatest enterprise of two centuries.''

The irony of the controversy was that while the public was focusing on underground lakes and flooded dams, the work itself was going far more smoothly than either Goethals or Sibert could possibly have hoped. Instead of being one of the most difficult jobs on the canal, as they had anticipated, it was turning out to be one of the most trouble-free. ''Gatun dam proved to be the happiest surprise of the whole waterway,'' remarked an observer.

In the spring of 1909, with the parallel-rock retaining walls of the eastern section finished and fill being pumped between them, the concrete spillway dam in the middle of the earthen dam began to take shape. The spillway dam, which was 808 feet long and 69 feet high, was a horseshoe-shaped structure with its outside curve to the lake and its inside curve facing downstream. Giant steel gates mounted between fourteen openings opened and closed like windows to regulate the water level of Gatun Lake. Any water from the lake that was released over the dam flowed into the 1200-foot-long concrete spillway and from there into the bed of the

Gatun's concrete dam and spillway are still under construction as late as 1913.

Chagres River, which resumed its course to the Atlantic Ocean at the bottom of the spillway. Because sudden rainstorms and freshets along the inland course of the Chagres River affected the level of Gatun Lake, observers stationed at intervals on the riverbanks periodically phoned in to the spillway operator to report on river conditions.

A hydroelectric power plant was built next to the spillway. Water dropping seventy-five feet from Gatun Lake through three huge penstocks (pipes) turned great turbines inside the plant that generated electricity for the canal locks, rock crushers, cement mixers, cranes, lighthouses and every village and town in the Zone. It was an all-electric canal, an amazing feat, considering that back in the United States many rural homes were still without electricity.

Next, all the trees and vegetation had to be cleared out of the channel that ships would eventually follow across Gatun Lake. This twenty-four-mile-long shipping channel, which would be from 500 to 1,000 feet wide, basically followed the original bed of the Chagres River. The area to be leveled was still so full of wildlife, Sibert noted that "monkeys chattered in protest as the timber was cut and the force performing this work actually killed a tiger cat with their machetes."

By the spring of 1910, the retaining walls of the eastern section had been completed, the shipping channel had been cleared and the native villages relocated (under great protest). The two parallel rock retaining walls for the western section had been built between the spillway dam and the west bank of the valley, with an eighty-foot-wide channel open in the middle through which the Chagres River still flowed. Now it was time to halt the flow of the river so that Gatun Lake could begin to fill up. The rainy season was about to begin and Sibert knew if the Chagres River wasn't dammed up soon, the river would flood so high, nothing would be able to stop its wild rush to the sea.

On April 22, 1910, Sibert ordered the railroad cars that were poised on trestles above the eighty-foot-wide channel to dump their loads of broken rock into the rushing river below. With a continuous stream of trains emptying rocks into the river, the two parallel rock walls began to rise slowly. But the river was rising too. Now half-ton rocks were being washed downstream by the

(Right) Dirt trains dump their loads of spoil in a last effort to stop the flow of the Chagres River, April 1910.

raging current. "It looked as if the Chagres were to be the winner in the fight," Sibert confessed later.

In desperation, he brought in carloads of rusted French railroad tracks and had them hurled into the river hoping that the rocks would catch in the rails and hold. He knew it was a risk. The rails, he said, "would result in either closing the river or tearing out the trestle." Suddenly there was a loud screech as the force of the river moved one of the trestles five feet downstream, threatening both the trestle and the train that was on it. Ignoring the danger, the train crew clambered down and added braces to the trestle. As soon as Sibert was sure the trestle was secure, he brought in more

trainloads of rock to dump into the river. This time the rusted railroad tracks caught the rocks and held them. The flow of the river was halted.

But Sibert's troubles weren't over. Only ten days later, water rushed through a huge hole in one of the western section's retaining walls, collapsing a trestle and washing out thousands of tons of fill. Although Sibert worked quickly to repair the damage, it took over a week to reset the trestle and build a dike to hold back the water.

And then, by the beginning of May it was over. The Chagres River was finally dammed across the western section so that Gatun Lake could begin to fill up, a process that would take almost four years. The currents of the Chagres River that entered the lake twenty-one miles from Gatun at Gamboa were now absorbed and made harmless by the sheer size of the lake.

Meanwhile, the process of pumping wet fill between the dam's retaining walls continued year after year. When the mile-and-a-half-long dam was at last finished in 1914, it contained nearly twenty-two million cubic yards of material. With one cubic yard of material filling a two-horse wagon, a contemporary writer noted that if all the material in the dam was "loaded into ordinary two-horse dirt wagons it would make a procession some 80,000 miles long" or more than three times around the equator.

Amazingly enough, the lush tropical growth that quickly grew over the finished dam made it look simply like a long sloping rise at one end of Gatun Lake. What appeared to be small islands scattered throughout the 164-square-mile lake were all that remained of the tops of jungle hills.

"The Gatun Dam was the keynote," John Stevens once said and he was right. In spite of all the criticism, rumors and hysteria, Gatun Dam, by creating a huge freshwater lake, had tamed the Chagres River forever. Instead of destroying the canal, the river now sustained its very life.

(Left) Wet fill is pumped between the retaining walls of Gatun Dam's eastern section, July 1911.

Ten

All the publicity that surrounded Culebra Cut and Gatun Dam totally overshadowed what was happening in the Pacific Division. And considering the problems there, it was probably just as well. The original plan for the Pacific Division called for one set of locks at the southern end of Culebra Cut at Pedro Miguel, man-made Sosa Lake, two sets of locks that projected into the Pacific at La Boca (Spanish for "the Mouth") and a four-mile-long channel across the Bay of Panama that extended into deep water in the Pacific.

As early as 1906 John Stevens protested that locks built right at the canal entrance couldn't be protected against enemy attack. Furthermore, he charged, there would be serious health problems "at the doors of Panama on account of mosquitoes and fever breeding." He wanted to build the locks four and a half miles farther inland, at Miraflores, and Secretary Taft agreed, saying, "It seems to me wiser to place the locks at Miraflores."

But the Board of Consulting Engineers had recommended La

Boca, pointing out that the subsoil "is firmer than we expected, and at the time of our visit, about two days after it had been flooded by spring tides, it could be walked on in most places." And so Congress passed into law plans that called for two locks and a dam at La Boca.

It didn't take long after work began on the dam in the fall of 1907 for both Goethals and Sydney B. Williamson, head of the Pacific Division, to realize that the La Boca site wasn't going to work out. The piles that were driven into the mud to support the railroad trestle for the dam settled so drastically that one train plunged right over the side. And the rock dumped into the mud for the dam's retaining walls caused huge hummocks to rise, first in one location and then in another. "In places this motion continued for two weeks after dumping had stopped," Goethals reported to Secretary Taft.

Immediately Goethals had more test pits and borings drilled, only to find that the subsoil was "blue clay without grit, possessing but little supporting power" on which neither a dam nor locks could be built. There was no question that the La Boca site had been a bad engineering blunder. Yet, incredibly, the entire problem was resolved by Goethals and President Roosevelt through the mail. In December of 1907, Roosevelt gave his approval (by letter) to Goethals's astounding request to move the two locks at La Boca four and a half miles inland to Miraflores where Stevens had wanted them in the first place.

The *Canal Record*'s announcement of this very major switch was brief: "On December 20, 1907 the President of the United States approved the plan which had been submitted by the Chairman and Chief Engineer [Goethals] for the change in location of the locks from La Boca to Miraflores."

Just as astonishing as the announcement itself was the fact that no sharp-eyed reporter picked up on it. And with Congress away on Christmas vacation, no gloomy Congressmen or team of experts traveled to Panama to shake their heads in dismay. The probable explanation for the amazing lack of publicity was that the Pacific Division had never sparked the public's imagination the way the other two divisions had. In fact, many still believe that three sets of locks at Miraflores similar to Gatun's three locks would have been an even better arrangement, although undoubtedly Goethals, Williamson and the engineering staff didn't want to draw any more attention to the locks than they already had by proposing yet another change.

Now, with the site moved to Miraflores, a ship entering Pedro Miguel's single set of locks from Culebra Cut would be lowered thirty feet to Miraflores Lake. The Rio Grande River and other small rivers flowing into the lake, as well as water from the operation of the Pedro Miguel locks above, would supply all the lake's fresh water. After crossing the mile-and-a-half-long lake, the ship would be lowered another fifty-five feet through Miraflores's two sets of locks to sea level. From there the ship would travel the final eight and a half miles of channel at sea level to deep water in the Pacific.

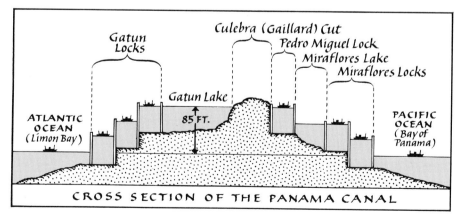
CROSS SECTION OF THE PANAMA CANAL

Work on the two dams at Pedro Miguel began in 1908, with a dam to be constructed on either side of Pedro Miguel's single set of locks. One dam connected the locks to the hills on the west and the other dam connected the locks to the hills on the east. Both dams also served as dikes so that water wouldn't be lost from Culebra Cut. The March 1909 *Canal Record* reported: "Compared to the great barrier that is being built across the Chagres Valley at Gatun, the Pedro Miguel dams are small, but are being constructed as carefully as Gatun dam itself."

"At Miraflores two dams are to be constructed," continued the *Canal Record*. As at Pedro Miguel, one dam connected the locks to the hills on the west and also acted as a dike to retain water in Miraflores Lake. The other dam, which connected the locks to the hills on the east, had a small concrete spillway dam built into it that would control the level of Miraflores Lake, just as Gatun's twice-as-large spillway dam would control the level of Gatun Lake. Any water released over the Miraflores spillway emptied into the canal just below the locks, and from there flowed at sea level out into the Pacific. A hydroelectric plant was constructed just south of the spillway to provide power needed for the construction and eventual operation of the Pacific Division's locks.

Because construction of the canal was never just one project, but many, many projects all going on at once, while work was continuing at Pedro Miguel and Miraflores, a shipping channel, 4 miles long and 500 feet wide, was being dredged in the Bay of Panama in the Pacific. To excavate the soft mud and blue clay of the bay, Williamson used just about every kind of floating dredge there was, suction dredges, dipper dredges, ladder dredges, even leftover French dredges that were salvaged from the harbor and repaired.

A sea-level channel also had to be excavated from the shoreline at the Bay of Panama four and a half miles inland to the locks at Miraflores. Because high and low tides in the Pacific differed as much as twenty feet, Goethals had an earthen dike built across the channel several miles in from the shoreline to keep out the waters of the Pacific so that steam shovels could do the excavating. When the excavation was almost finished, Goethals had a second dike constructed about a mile farther inland from the first. Billions of gallons of water were then pumped into the basin created by the two dikes to allow floating dredges to complete the excavation. When the channel had been dug to its final depth of 45 feet and width of 500 feet, the earthen dikes were dynamited out and salt-water from the Pacific was released into the channel as far as the locks at Miraflores.

Because strong Pacific crosscurrents dumped tons of sand and silt at the canal entrance, a permanent dike, or breakwater, had to be built out into the Bay of Panama to prevent the canal entrance from getting clogged. When the breakwater was finished, it would extend from La Boca across the bay over three miles out to Naos Island in the Pacific. The breakwater would also serve as a bridge between the mainland and Naos Island, as well as nearby Flamenco and Perico islands.

To build the Naos breakwater, Goethals had a trestle constructed across the bay from which trains could dump their loads of spoil. But as soon as work began, the same greasy blue clay that had created such problems at La Boca now caused whole sections of trestle to sink and slip out of place. However, because the breakwater was absolutely essential to the Pacific entrance of the canal, this time there could be no changing locations or giving up. Goethals had no choice but to keep adding more spoil. After more than three years, not one section of trestle was where it had originally been built and the breakwater was still a mile short of Naos

Goethals [in white shirt] inspects the hummocks that heave up in the Bay of Panama as more rocks are dumped onto the Naos breakwater, February 1914.

Island. In the end, ten times more spoil was needed to finish the breakwater than had originally been estimated.

While all this construction was going on in the Pacific Division, similar work was taking place at the other end of the canal in the Atlantic Division where a 500-foot-wide shipping channel 4 miles long and 41 feet deep was being dredged out of Limon Bay. Another 500-foot-wide channel was also being excavated from the Limon Bay shoreline 3 miles inland to the Gatun locks. Because the difference between high and low tides in the Atlantic was only about a foot, water was simply released from the bay into the channel so that dredges could do the work, with dynamite and steam shovels needed for only one short section that was solid rock.

With violent Atlantic storms making Limon Bay a dangerous

The Atlantic Ocean pounds at the Toro Point breakwater as a steel plow unloads rocks from the one-sided dirt cars.

harbor for ships, a two-mile-long breakwater had to be constructed out from the shoreline at Toro Point into deep water. The breakwater, which also prevented sand and silt from choking up the canal entrance, was constructed by dumping stone into the sea, driving piles into the stone and then laying railroad tracks on top of the stone wall, from which more stone was dumped. To protect the harbor more fully, a second, shorter breakwater was built later.

Inland, gangs of workers were relocating miles of Panama Railroad tracks that the creation of Gatun Lake would soon flood. Moving the tracks was a logistical nightmare that took five years and cost nearly $9 million. Goethals wrote in 1911, ''One of the most difficult tasks connected with the canal is to relocate and rebuild the Panama Railroad, and at the same time not to interfere with the tremendous traffic across the Isthmus.''

And ''tremendous'' was the right word. Every day, 600 trains moved passengers, supplies, mail, money, freight and dirt, with dirt trains having the right of way over all other trains except for a train on which the president of the United States might be travel-

(Right) The relocation of the Panama Railroad takes time, money and manpower.

ing. Although the Panama Railroad had only been 47 and a half miles long when it was first built, during the construction years, over 200 miles of track were laid in the Central Division alone, so that when the canal was finished, about all that was left of the original railroad was its name.

While all this drama was being enacted, less dramatic but no less important construction was taking place. Complete towns of homes, schools, churches, stores, post offices and clubhouses were springing up all along the canal route. Spoil from Culebra Cut was dumped into the marshy swampland near the Pacific entrance at La Boca to create the future capital of the Zone. With the cities of Cristóbal and Colón (Christopher Columbus) honoring Columbus at the Atlantic entrance, it seemed fitting to honor the discoverer of the Pacific by changing the name La Boca to Balboa at the Pacific entrance.

Terminals went up at either end of the canal, as well as facilities that would one day be handling thousands of ships a year—wharves, docks, piers, storehouses, dry docks and machine shops. Although crude oil was being used increasingly for fuel, with coal still the primary fuel for ships, heating plants, steam shovels and other canal machinery, huge coaling stations had to be built. The design and construction of these facilities was under the supervision of Admiral Harry Rousseau, the only Navy man to serve on the Commission.

After lengthy debate about whether or not the canal should be neutral, Congress finally decided to fortify the canal from both sea and land attack. A system of submarine mines was established near both canal entrances, with forts constructed on Naos, Flamenco and Perico islands in the Pacific, and forts and gun emplacements located on the Atlantic. When construction of the canal began in 1904, attack from the air wasn't even a possibility, although as early as 1912 a farsighted writer noted, "Against the miraculous, such as the presence of an aeroplane with an operator so skilled as to drop bombs upon a target of less than 40 feet square, no defense could fully prevail."

Although the construction of the Panama Canal, from its dams to its breakwaters to housing for the workers, was a multilayered and complex engineering effort, without question, the design and building of its six sets of locks was *the* technical achievement of the entire project.

Eleven

In a 1910 speech to canal employees, President Taft made a reference to the locks. "Gatun and Miraflores and Pedro Miguel were sleeping peacefully, with no knowledge of the world-wide reputation that they were subsequently to acquire." Certainly any worldwide reputation the locks acquired was well deserved. According to Major Sibert, "No such massive walls of concrete had been built as those designed for the locks of the Panama Canal." Five city blocks long and higher than a six-story building, a lock, if turned on end, would have been the tallest structure in the world. It was no wonder that the locks, which were designed by Commission member Colonel Harry Hodges, took almost four years to build.

The six sets of locks on the canal, three at Gatun, one at Pedro Miguel and two at Miraflores, were identical. Each lock had side-by-side chambers so that two ships could be locked through at the same time. One of Goethals's most far-reaching decisions as chief engineer was to widen the lock chambers from 95 feet to 110 feet

Men and machines are dwarfed by the size of a lock.

and lengthen them from 900 feet to 1,000 feet. Although Goethals upgraded the size of the locks to accommodate the battleships the Navy was planning to build at the time, the added size has enabled the huge ships of today to lock through as well.

Because the locks were to be from seventy to eighty feet deep, thousands and thousands of cubic yards of dirt and rocks had to be excavated from the lock sites. For more than two years, gangs of workers did nothing but drill, blast and remove spoil so that it wasn't until 1909 that actual construction of the locks began.

All the lock walls, floors and approach walls were built of concrete, a combination of sand, gravel and portland cement (portland cement itself being a mixture of limestone and clay). The two side-by-side lock chambers shared a sixty-foot-wide center wall with the side wall in each chamber forty-five feet wide at the bottom narrowing in a series of steps to eight feet wide at the top. Although in those days concrete was usually reinforced, that is, strengthened by adding metal rods, it was now decided that all the concrete in the locks, except for the lock floors, would not be reinforced. Because the locks have been in daily use since 1914 and because Panama's climate is so punishing, today's engineers are astounded that what was basically experimental concrete is still in near-perfect condition.

Both the sand and rock for the concrete were quarried locally, with the rock crushed into gravel at two large crushing plants. Although the engineers had found perfect quality sand on Panama's San Blas Islands in the Atlantic, the Cuna Indian chief there refused to sell it in the belief that everything on the islands was a gift from God and not for sale . . . especially to white men. As for the cement, it all had to be shipped from the United States, a total of over four and a half million barrels during the construction years.

Once the excavation of the lock sites was finished at Gatun in the Atlantic Division, the concrete work could begin. Sand and gravel were brought up the old French canal by barge to Gatun and unloaded into storage piles. Small electric railroad cars then picked up the correct ratio of sand, gravel and cement and delivered them to concrete mixers located inside the locks. After water was added and the materials mixed, the wet concrete was poured out the opposite side of the mixers into two huge buckets set on flat cars. Another small electric railroad ran the two buckets over to one of the eight cableways that were suspended between high towers located on either side of the locks. The buckets of concrete, which weighed as much as six tons, were attached to hooks and

Major Sibert surveys his tower-and-cableway system at Gatun.

swung through the air on the cableway. When the buckets reached their destination, they were lowered and the concrete was poured into huge steel molds where men working knee-deep in the wet concrete spread it. Both the steel molds and the eighty-five-foot-high towers that supported the cableways were on tracks that could be moved forward as each thirty-six-foot-long section of lock was finished, a process that took about a week.

A totally different system of delivering concrete to the steel molds was used for the Pedro Miguel and Miraflores locks in the Pacific Division. Because these locks were located in a narrow valley with hills on either side, the Gatun tower-and-cableway system, which required open space, simply wasn't possible. Instead, huge steel cranes handled all the concrete.

At Pedro Miguel, four berm cranes that traveled on tracks outside the locks on the berm, or bank, of the canal, were operated from an engine house located on the crane itself. On either side of the engine house was a 350-foot-long arm that supported a traveling trolley from which a huge bucket hung. The operator in the crane's engine house dropped the empty bucket by trolley down to stockpiles where it picked up the correct amount of sand and rock. Still traveling by trolley, the bucket was next swung over to bins where cement was added, and from there the materials were delivered to the concrete mixers.

After water was added and the materials mixed, the wet con-

(Top left) Wet concrete is poured into buckets set on flatcars at the Gatun lock site. (Bottom left) The buckets of wet concrete are delivered to cableways that hang between movable towers.

At Pedro Miguel, mixers located under the arm of the berm crane discharge wet concrete into waiting buckets.

crete was poured into buckets and transported by small railroad cars to four chamber cranes located inside the lock chambers. There the buckets were hooked onto cables that were attached to the crane's arms, raised into the air and sent to the proper steel mold. As at Gatun, the concrete was poured from the buckets into the steel molds where workers spread it around.

At the Miraflores locks, there were two berm cranes, one on the east bank and one on the west. The storage piles of sand, gravel and cement, as well as the cement mixers, were all under one arm of the crane. Once the concrete was mixed and poured into buckets set on flatcars, an electric railroad delivered the buckets to the other arm of the crane, which in turn dumped the concrete directly into the steel molds. Later, chamber cranes were brought from Pedro Miguel and installed inside the Miraflores lock chambers so that larger amounts of concrete could be handled at one time.

(Right) At Miraflores, both berm and chamber cranes handle the concrete that is being poured into 36-foot-long steel molds.

"The four chamber cranes are designed to pick up the buckets, deliver them to the lock walls, dump their concrete and return the empties to the cars at a combined average rate of 320 cubic yards of concrete an hour," wrote Pacific Division's Sydney Williamson who had originated the crane system, just as Atlantic Division's William Sibert had originated the cableway system at Gatun.

Actually the design of the cranes was so practical, the trolley-and-bucket arrangement was used for lifting or moving just about anything, from a dozen workers to sections of railroad track. It was a mammoth erector set of robot arms swinging immense buckets through the air, with high steel towers and giant pyramids of concrete dwarfing the electric trains. And the chamber cranes were so tall, they could be seen for miles, with the operator perched nearly a hundred feet up in the air in a tiny box that hung from one of the crane's arms.

The sounds were equally spectacular: rattling locomotives, grinding concrete mixers, squealing cables and the thunder of crushed rock being dumped. "The most monumental piece of work on the Canal, and the most pictorial," declared artist Joseph Pennell who had traveled to Panama to sketch the canal under construction.

The design of the locks was as ingenious as the design of the cranes. With Gatun Lake the main source of water for the canal, gravity moved all the water in and out of the locks without the need for a single pump. In the Atlantic Division at Gatun, fresh water flowed into the top set of locks from Gatun Lake and from there flowed down into the next two sets of locks by gravity. In

(Above) The main culverts through which water flows in and out of the lock chambers are 18 feet in diameter. (Right) The main culverts are constructed with collapsible steel forms that are moved forward as the lock chambers take shape.

the Pacific Division, Pedro Miguel's one set of locks, which was filled with water from Culebra Cut (an extension of Gatun Lake), emptied directly into Miraflores Lake. At the Miraflores locks, fresh water from Miraflores Lake filled the top set of locks which in turn flowed down into the second set of locks. At both Gatun and Miraflores, the water simply drained from the bottom locks into the sea-level channels and from there out to sea.

Water entered a lock chamber through huge tunnels, or culverts, built into the walls of the lock chambers, one main culvert in the center wall and one main culvert in each of the side walls. From these culverts, the water flowed into smaller cross culverts built under the chamber floor, ten coming out at right angles from the culvert in the center wall and ten coming out at right angles from the culvert in the side wall. There were five holes in each of these twenty cross culverts through which the

water bubbled up into the chamber. Because there were so many holes in the floor (100), the water flowed into the chamber smoothly, without any turbulence that might damage a ship or the chamber itself.

When the water level in the chamber was being lowered, the water drained out the floor holes into the cross culverts and from there out through the main culverts. The sheer size of the culverts was mind-boggling. The main culverts were eighteen feet in diameter, large enough for a railroad car to drive through, the cross culverts were six and a half feet by eight feet, a comfortable fit for a wagon and two horses while each of the 100 holes in the floor was four and a half feet in diameter.

A lock chamber is the same height as a six-story building. The steps of the lock will be filled in later with earth and stone and graded to the top.

The valves that admitted or released water through the main culverts into the chambers were sliding steel gates run by electricity. These valve gates, each weighing ten tons, opened and closed like windows. To fill the lock chamber with water so that a ship could be raised to the next level, the valve gates at the lower end of the chamber were closed and the valve gates at the upper end were opened. To lower a ship, the process was reversed.

To admit a ship into a lock chamber, huge miter gates swung

(Right) Because the Pacific tides vary as much as 20 feet, the 82-foot-high Miraflores sea-level gates are the tallest on the canal. Steel plates will later be riveted onto the gates' hollow frames.

open like double doors and wheeled back into the lock walls. Once the ship was in the lock, the miter gates swung shut. These miter gates were made up of two leaves that were each sixty-five feet wide, seven feet thick and weighed hundreds of tons. They were so huge, the hinges that fastened the gates to the walls weighed fourteen tons each. Despite their size, the miter gates were hollow and watertight and actually floated once water was in the locks.

As a safety feature, the leaves of the gates were designed to close in a V, with the V always pointing upstream against the

downward pressure of the water. Only when the water pressure on both sides of the gates was equal, that is, the level of the water was the same on both sides of the gates, could the gates be opened or closed. An additional safety feature was a second set of gates constructed at each end of the uppermost lock that was identical to the set of main gates. These gates would be used only in case the main gates didn't work properly or were rammed by an out-of-control ship.

Another set of gates, called intermediate gates, was constructed in each lock chamber. By leaving the main gates open and using

only the intermediate gates, the length of the lock chamber could be shortened from 1,000 feet to 600 feet. Considering that a ship that required the full 1,000-foot length of the lock used 52 million gallons of fresh water in its passage through the canal (a day's supply of water for a city the size of Des Moines), the intermediate gates provided an enormous saving of water. The main, safety and intermediate gates, a total of forty-six sets of gates, were opened and closed electrically by steel arms connected to seventeen-ton "bull" wheels built inside the lock walls. Despite the size of the gates, they were so delicately balanced, they could be opened or closed silently and with no vibration in about two minutes by a forty-horsepower electric motor.

The gates were constructed by riveting a steel plate to a grid of steel girders just the way a modern plane wing is riveted. While standing on tiny platforms or dangling from swinging scaffolds seventy-five feet in the air, the riveters had to catch red-hot rivets in a bucket and then quickly rivet them in with an air gun while the rivets were still hot. It was a risky job.

A former riveter remembered the danger only too well: "When I look I saw this man down below. The scaffold break away with him and he went right down. And this plank down there with a spike and the spike went right through his skull. . . . Riveters, man, they used to die everyday." Danger or not, every one of the six million rivets needed for the lock gates was inspected. "A white man, with a white suit, and a white hat come down with a little tinker hammer. He checked every rivet," another riveter recalled.

Safety in the locks was the keynote. The assistant chief engineer announced, "There is to be provided above each lock an emergency dam, which can be closed in case of accidents." These emergency dams functioned like a movable bridge that could

(Left) The huge "bull" wheels inside the lock walls that open and close the gates are operated by a 40-horsepower motor.

swing out over the lock and lower gates quickly to cut off any unexpected flow of water.

Another safety feature was a twelve-ton iron fender chain that ran between the chamber walls. If the ship was proceeding normally, the chain was lowered into a special groove in the chamber floor. In the remote chance that the ship was out of control, an automatic mechanism would release the chain until the ship was stopped.

As for the actual transit, plans called for a canal pilot, or pilots, to board the ship in deep water. With the actual captain of the ship lacking all authority, the canal pilot (or pilots) navigated the ship through the entire length of the canal until the ship reached deep water at the other end.

Every set of locks had a 1,000-foot-long concrete approach wall at either end (the total length of Gatun's three locks was over a mile). As soon as a ship drew even with the approach wall, line

handlers threw lines from the deck that were connected to electrically operated locomotives called mules. These mules, which had identical cabs front and back so that they could go in either direction, ran on tracks built into the top of the lock walls, with four mules usually assigned to each ship. Two mules, one on either side of the lock, were attached to the bow of the ship to tow it, while two more mules, one on either side of

An electric mule travels down the lock wall past the Gatun control house.

Once the electric switchboard in the control house is completed, one operator will be able to direct the entire passage of a ship through a set of locks.

the lock, were attached to the stern of the ship to brake it. The mules also served to keep the ship centered in the lock so that neither the ship nor the lock would be damaged.

Each of the three sets of locks was operated electrically by a switchboard that was housed in a building located on the lock's center wall. The switchboard, designed by the brand-new General Electric Company, was operated by one person who could direct the entire passage of a ship through each set of locks, from opening and closing the gates to controlling the water level to lowering the fender chain. Every mechanism in the locks was reproduced in miniature on the sixty-five-foot-long switchboard so that simply by turning what looked like a water-faucet handle, the operator could raise or lower a ship through a lock chamber even if the motor being turned on was half a mile away. Because the switches

With spectators lining the approach walls, the tugboat Gatun *enters Gatun's lower lock, September 26, 1913.*

all interlocked, they had to be operated in the right sequence in order to work.

The single set of locks at Pedro Miguel was finished in 1911, with the double set at Miraflores and the triple set at Gatun both completed in 1913, a year earlier than Goethals had estimated. On September 26, 1913, an old tug, appropriately named *Gatun*, was cleaned up and draped with flags for a trial run through Gatun's three locks. Colonel Goethals followed the *Gatun*'s progress from the sidelines, along with the thousands of spectators who showed up to watch. It was a long, hot day, but when the *Gatun* finally made it up through all three locks, the crowds went wild. They had witnessed an historical event and they knew it.

"Since all the locks are similar in structure this test was a test for all locks. A test of the locks meant a test of the Canal," declared Major Sibert. Not only had the locks worked, they had worked perfectly. And in contrast to the deafening noise of construction, they had worked in complete silence. Their design and construction were an engineering triumph in the creative use of electricity, steel and concrete. It was a canal that couldn't have been built even ten years earlier.

Technical achievement that the locks certainly were, perhaps an equally great achievement was the human effort that produced them. After the canal was finished, only a handful of employees returned home famous, while the thousands and thousands who made up the vast majority will be forever nameless. Nameless or not, they were a courageous band who risked everything in a strange land and without whom the construction of the Panama Canal would never have been possible.

Twelve

Although an amazing number of men and women worked on the canal during the construction years—well over 100,000—the average stay for an American was only about a year. The *Canal Record* noted, "From the beginning of American occupation the problem was not so much to obtain men as to keep them on the work after they had been brought here."

To encourage Americans to remain on the Isthmus, first Stevens and then Goethals did everything possible to improve their living conditions. They saw to it that the Commission provided free housing, utilities, medical, maid and janitor services, as well as nine paid holidays a year, a forty-two-day vacation and thirty days of sick leave. For recreation, the Commission sponsored Saturday night dances, sports, movies, concerts, fraternal organizations and hobby clubs. An employee was quoted in the *Canal Record* as saying, "Everything is done to make it as pleasant as possible for the men and I have not seen a man that was not satisfied."

Eighteen commissaries owned by the Panama Railroad sold all kinds of goods, from flour to children's shoes to pianos, at about one-third the cost of back home. Cash was never exchanged. "All purchases are made with coupons issued by the Commission and charged against the employee's salary account," explained the *Canal Record.*

Like Stevens before him, Goethals believed that married men stabilized the work force and it was true that married men stayed longer on the Isthmus than bachelors, although as late as 1912 only about one American worker in four was married. Single men lived in quarters with twelve to sixty other men, two men to a room, while married men were assigned housing according to their salaries. To encourage employees to work harder for promotion, the higher their pay was, the better their housing and benefits were. Harry Franck, a young census taker, wrote in 1912: "Every rank and shade of man has a different salary, and exactly in accordance with that salary is he housed, furnished and treated down to the last item—number of electric lights, style of bed, size of bookcase."

The average pay for an American worker was $150 a month, with nurses and teachers earning $60, locomotive engineers from $180 to $210 and steam-shovel engineers $310, all about twenty-five percent higher than salaries back home. Married men who earned less than $200 a month (the majority) lived in four-family houses; a $200- to $300-a-month salary rated a two-family house; $300- to $400-a-month employees were assigned to two-story houses, while $400 a month or more merited "large houses of a type distinguished by spaciousness and artistic design."

Salaries not only dictated housing, but Zone social life as well. "Caste lines are as sharply drawn as in India," commented Franck. "Mrs. X., whose husband is foreman at $165, would not think of

More-than-adequate housing is provided for Major Gaillard who is a member of the Commission and head of the Central Division.

playing cards with Mrs. Y., whose husband gets $150." With the *Canal Record* publishing a weekly list of what food was available on which days of the week for how much, it was hard to be original. A young wife complained, "What's the good of giving a dinner party, when your guests all know exactly what everything on your table costs, and they can guess just what you are going to serve?"

But Zone conformity went deeper than what was being served for dinner. "The Canal Zone is not a democracy," stated Willis Abbot. "It has no constitution so far as its residents are concerned. There are no elections and no elected officials." The Commission, under Goethals, controlled the police, schools, post office, fire department, courts and even owned most of the churches. The only trials by jury (three-man juries, at that) involved the death sentence or life imprisonment, with judges ruling on all other cases. In 1912 alone, over 7,000 arrests were made, with a seventy percent conviction rate. The *Canal Record* described how Zone roads were built by convicts. "The felons work with ball and chain, and with at least one guard to each ten prisoners."

The Commission's virtual dictatorship over every phase of Zone life went mostly unnoticed by outsiders who only saw well-dressed, cheerful Americans who appeared to be carefree. "There are no hard times on the Zone, no hurried, worried faces, no famished wolfish eyes," wrote Franck. Nevertheless, there were critics who described Zone society as "governmental parenthood" . . . "modern socialism" . . . "a narrow ribbon of standardized buildings and standarized men working at standardized jobs" . . . "a drearily efficient state."

Drearily efficient or not, workers managed to find their own means of escape. Panama City and Colón, which were lined with bars and gambling halls, "served as a sort of safety valve, where a man can . . . get rid of the bad eternal vapors that might cause an explosion in a ventless society," Franck said. But the Big Job held top priority on the Isthmus and canal officials were never very happy with the temptations that Panama nightlife offered. The chief of police made Commission policy plain: "We want all the laborers fit and hearty for work when the morning whistle blows."

Because most Americans felt a sense of pride in their contribution to the project, a tale to be handed down to grandchildren, they didn't object to the rules and restrictions. "We owe it to our country to make whatever sacrifices the work demands," was how one worker expressed it. Another said, "I felt that I was having part and parcel of the greatest enterprise of all the ages." A staff engineer wrote later, "Every man was proud to be a member of the force."

To honor employees who had spent two or more years on the canal, President Roosevelt had medals minted from copper, bronze and tin scraps salvaged from old French equipment. On one side was a portrait of Roosevelt and on the other was a ship sailing through Culebra Cut with the worker's name engraved under it.

The only Americans who had no role to play in the unfolding

drama were the enlisted men in the Army and Marines who were a presence on the Isthmus from the beginning. With a base salary of eighteen dollars a month and no Commission advantages, they sweated out their three-year tour of duty on the fringes of history-in-the-making.

Still, even the enlisted men fared better than the black employees, for whom nothing much had changed since Wallace's time. Although census taker Franck reported in 1912 that sixty-eight countries were represented, with large numbers from Spain and Italy, most of the unskilled labor force came from the West Indies. Almost without exception the West Indians were a gentle, law-abiding, sober and religious people, with an unusually low crime rate.

Although the work force drew from Jamaica, Martinique and other West Indian islands, most of the unskilled labor came from Barbados, nearly 20,000 workers, or about forty percent of the entire Barbadian male population. A former worker recalled the high unemployment rate in Barbados during those years: "I wanted to get out . . . in Barbados they wasn't paying you nothing. And even ten cents an hour to come to Panama was better than to stay in Barbados."

The ten-cents-an-hour was standard pay for a ten-hour day, six days a week. As late as 1909, an order from Goethals read: "The maximum rate for West Indian laborers is 10 cents per hour. The 16-cent and 20-cent rate are for European, other white, and black American laborers only." Granted, a contract with the Commission did guarantee free passage back home but only after the employee had worked a total of 500 days.

A rough four- or five-day trip by overcrowded steamer brought the West Indian recruit to Colón, where he was vaccinated, given a tin plate and cup and a brass tag with a number on

A boat crowded with recruits arrives in Colón harbor from Barbados.

it called a check. The check, which controlled every phase of a worker's life from then on, was needed to collect pay, obtain coupon books and receive a meal, not to mention identifying its owner in case of death.

The first fact the black worker learned on his arrival was that the Commission ran a totally segregated operation—housing, schools, churches, commissaries, railroad cars, mess halls and recreational facilities, right down to every pay line, drinking fountain, post office window and toilet. Because only white skilled

Separate Gold and Silver lines form as pay cars roll into Culebra Cut.

American workers were paid in gold and black unskilled workers were paid in Panamanian silver coins called balboas (which had half the value of the gold), the terms "Gold" and "Silver" soon became the segregating device. Secretary Taft reinforced the system in 1908 when he issued an order that only Americans could be hired as gold-roll employees. "The brilliant idea occurred to someone in the early days," was the offensive comment of a contemporary (white) writer.

Years later former West Indian workers were still bitter.

"That discrimination came about by Americans . . . to keep Negroes apart from the white people. And that was through the Canal Zone in its entirety."

"You couldn't drink water in a white man fountain. You see it says . . . White, White."

"The Gold was the white and the Silver was the Negro. And when the Negro getting ten cents an hour, the Gold is getting thirty or forty cents."

(Right) Gold and Silver entrances are clearly marked at the Balboa commissary.

To give some idea as to numbers of workers, 1,600 pounds of gold were paid out each month to Gold employees, while 24 tons of silver were paid to unskilled black workers. During the last years of construction, there were 40,000 black employees as compared to less than 6,000 Americans and their dependents. Visitors arriving in Panama who thought that the canal was being built by white Americans were usually astounded at the number of black workers. And understandably so. Back home almost no mention or credit was given to the black work force in newspapers, speeches or in Congress. The *Canal Record* took little notice of them either. With lengthy obituaries for every American death, black deaths rated only a line or two. "Percy O'Neil, a Jamaican, Check No. 71,824, was fatally injured at Gatun on September 1," was one such typical *Canal Record* account.

Unfortunately, housing for single black men under Goethals wasn't much better than it had ever been, that is, either makeshift barracks that housed seventy-two men to a room with outside toilets and washhouses, or converted boxcars that were moved along the railroad line according to where workers were needed. The few quarters available to married Silver employees were two rooms in

barracks that housed five to eight other families. No quarters at all were provided for the West Indian women who came to the Isthmus to join a family member or simply to earn more money than they could at home.

Not surprisingly, thousands of West Indians constructed their own shacks of tin, dynamite cartons or dry goods boxes in the jungle or found what housing they could afford in the slums of Colón and Panama City. Joseph Bishop later wrote, "The great majority of the negroes preferred a shack in the jungle to the clean and airy quarters which the Commission offered free." A former Silver worker had a different viewpoint: "I could never live comfortable in those places. So, that's why myself and my uncle, he was alive, and another fellow, we went and rent outside room."

Dining services were segregated, too. Gold employees were well fed in dining halls for thirty cents a meal, while European laborers ate at sit-down messes that cost forty cents for three meals. The black workers, who had twenty-seven cents a day deducted from their pay for three meals, were served cafeteria-style in mess kitchens and ate standing up. "Each laborer had his little kit into which his meal was put, and he could carry it anywhere he desired to eat it," reported the *Canal Record.* Needless to say, many of the West Indians prepared their own meals.

Little organized recreation existed for blacks. Of the $2,500,000 that the Commission spent annually on recreation, each unskilled married black worker averaged $50 worth of benefits, while each married white worker averaged $750. Although there were twice as many black school children as white, there were less than half as many black teachers. The 90 West Indians on the Zone police force (out of a total of 300) only received half pay and weren't eligible for promotion.

Medical care was free to all employees and their families but, like everything else, it was segregated and definitely not equal. Because so many West Indians lived in the bush or in slums, they were especially prone to disease. "No attempt was made to screen all the barracks and shacks that housed the workers," reported Willis Abbot, which undoubtedly was a factor in the high number of malaria cases among black workers.

From the beginning of work until the end, disease and accidents took 5,609 lives, 4,500 of whom were black and 350 of whom were white Americans. West Indian workers never forgot the twin perils of danger and disease that they faced: "Thank God I am yet alive" . . . "Many time I meet death at the door" . . . "I thank God because I could have been dead several times."

Unfortunately, the prejudice that the West Indians suffered was a reflection of the times and because they weren't American citizens, they had no political vote or voice in Washington that might have brought about change. But despite their problems, work in the Zone did have some benefits. Although the jobs were often dangerous, Commission safety regulations were stricter than any back in the United States at that time. Because the commissary prices were rock-bottom, adequate food was always available and the West Indians for the most part earned more money than they could have in the islands, enough so that many sent for their wives and children or helped support families back home.

They were awarded no medals, but like the Americans, they, too, took pride in what they were doing. "Most of us came from our homelands in search of work and improvements. We turned out to be pioneers in a foreign land," recalled a Barbadian. "My greatest experience was the construction of the Panama Canal," declared one former worker, while another said, "Oh, yes. I mean the experience that I gained on the canal, I am very proud of it."

And well they all might have been.

Thirteen

Incredibly, the work was basically finished six months ahead of schedule. By the end of September 1913, the last of Gatun Dam's spillway gates was closed and the locks were completed. And then, on October 1, 1913, a violent twenty-five-second-long earthquake that registered Six on the Richter scale jolted the Isthmus, cracking walls in Panama City, destroying a church and causing a woman's death by heart attack. Although aftershocks continued for twelve days, the canal passed nature's ultimate test with flying colors. "There has been no damage whatever to any part of the canal," reported the *Canal Record.*

Only nine days after the earthquake, on October 10, 1913, President Woodrow Wilson pressed a button in Washington that relayed a signal to Panama. Seconds later dynamite charges went off in the earthen dike that had been built at the northern end of Culebra Cut at Gamboa to hold back the Chagres River. Although six pumps had slowly been releasing water into Culebra Cut, this was the dramatic moment. With a rush, the river poured through

Workers load dynamite into 42-foot-deep holes on Gamboa Dike, October 8, 1913.

the hole into the nine-mile Cut. It had been almost four hundred years to the day that Balboa had sighted the Pacific and now the Atlantic and Pacific were joined! A worker's wife later recalled, "Seeing Gamboa Dike blown up was a lot more than a big explosion—it was seeing what was accomplished; it was writing finis to the job."

Actually, it wasn't until December 10, after dredges had cleared out more mud slides at Cucaracha, that water began to fill the canal from end to end. But with water in the canal, all the intricate and complex mechanisms disappeared from sight. A staff member later wrote, "As is the case with very many engineering enterprises, the real and important work is buried in and underneath the completed structure."

Although Goethals always insisted that once the canal was finished the slides in the Cut would be "overcome finally and for all time" he was wrong. Slides have been a continuous problem ever since the canal opened, with a slide in 1915 that closed the canal for more than half a year and another as late as 1974 that limited traffic to one-way for months. Dredges, in fact, have removed more spoil from the canal since 1914 than the 232 million cubic yards that were removed during the entire ten years of construction.

Just as Goethals completed the canal early, so he also brought it in under the estimated cost. The final total, which came to something over $370 million, included purchase of both Panamanian and French rights and holdings, relocation of the Panama Railroad, sanitation expenses and all construction (Culebra Cut alone cost $90 million). What was almost as amazing was that the Commission had contracts for supplies with several thousand different manufacturers and yet no hint of graft or kickbacks have ever come to light, a tribute indeed to the high ethical standards

that George Goethals set as Commission chairman.

And the finished canal had an innate functional beauty. Appointed in 1912 to make artistic recommendations to the president, a Commission of Fine Arts chaired by the sculptor Daniel Chester French and the landscape architect Frederick L. Olmsted, Jr., reported: "There is little to find fault with from the artist's point of view. The Canal, like the pyramids, or some imposing object in natural scenery, is impressive from its scale and simplicity and directness."

Now, with the canal finished, it was time for the employees to move on to other construction and manufacturing jobs. Some left for Alaska, others for the new automobile industry in Detroit, while still others signed up for projects abroad. Although many West Indians returned to their home islands, a good number decided to stay on in Panama.

In January 1914, President Wilson disbanded the Commission, named Goethals as the first governor of the Panama Canal Zone at a salary of $10,000 ($5,000 less than he'd made as chief engineer) and announced plans for a gala opening of the canal to be held January 1, 1915. But in August 1914, World War I exploded in Europe and instead of one hundred international warships transiting from the Atlantic to the Pacific, on August 15, 1914, a sturdy cement carrier, the S.S. *Ancon*, made the first official passage. With the crisis in Europe filling the newspapers, the opening of the canal rated only a mention on the back pages. *The New York Times* simply announced, "The Panama Canal is open to the commerce of the world. Henceforth ships may pass to and fro through that great waterway."

But to Colonel Goethals it was no back-page event. Although he never revealed his thoughts, after devoting seven years of his life to the canal, he must have felt a sense of victory as he fol-

(Left) Dredging in the canal never ends.

Water bubbles up from the chamber floor as the S.S. Ancon *is towed through Gatun's lower lock on August 15, 1914.*

lowed the *Ancon's* progress across the Isthmus in the Yellow Peril. Certainly many others deserve credit, especially John Stevens, but it was Goethals's engineering ability, personal integrity and determination that had brought the canal to a successful completion.

Back home there was no question about who deserved the credit. Columbia, Harvard and Yale universities awarded Goethals honorary degrees and his name was even mentioned as a possible presidential candidate. Teddy Roosevelt wrote, "Colonel Goethals proved to be the man of all others to do the job. It would be impossible to overstate what he has done." Goethals returned the compliment. "The real builder of the canal was Theodore Roosevelt," he wrote. "It could not have been more of a personal triumph if he had personally lifted every shovelful of earth in its construction."

History, too, has always credited Teddy Roosevelt with the Panama Canal, and rightly so, but William Howard Taft, who traveled seven times to the Isthmus during the construction years, was also a powerful influence, first as Secretary of War from 1904 to 1908 and then as president from 1909 to 1913. Woodrow Wilson hadn't been in office long when the canal was finished in 1914 and although he had little impact on construction, it was he who formally opened the canal by proclamation in 1920.

Of necessity, many changes have been made since the *Ancon's* maiden voyage. Culebra Cut has been widened as well as renamed Gaillard Cut after Central Division's Major David Gaillard who died in 1913. Because of the need for better visibility and the threat of more slides, some of the hills in the Cut have been lowered or cut back. In 1935 Madden Dam and Power Project was constructed nine miles above Gamboa to further control the Chagres River floodwaters, create a twenty-two-square-mile lake to store water for the dry season and produce additional electric power.

Channel lighting was added in 1966 to allow ships to use the canal twenty-four hours a day, with high mast lighting installed recently to increase night visibility. Other modern improvements include a closed-circuit TV system, high-frequency radio channels, computerized traffic control and new, more powerful tugboats. With the increased size of modern ships, up to eight mules (new Japanese locomotives have replaced the original electric mules) are now needed for towing, braking and guiding ships through the locks. Inventive as they were at the time, the emergency dams and fender chains are no longer in use.

The mile-long Bridge of the Americas was built over the canal to connect Panama City and Balboa with the west side of the canal, as well as to serve as a link in the Pan-American Highway. Another bridge spans the Chagres River at Gamboa, and a highway has been constructed across the Isthmus between Panama City and Colón. A problem that still needs to be resolved is that traditional Panamanian slash-and-burn farming techniques and the destruction of forest areas for lumber have resulted in soil erosion and runoff, which in turn have seriously damaged the canal's watershed areas and caused heavy silting in Gatun and Madden lakes.

In an attempt to handle increased traffic, Congress appropriated $277,000 in 1939 to construct another set of locks with chambers 140 feet wide and 1,200 feet long. Although excavation was begun in 1940 on what was called the Third Locks Project, World War II intervened and work has never been resumed. As for the workers, "Gold" and "Silver" labels were changed to "United States rate" and "local rate" in 1947, but actual segregation didn't end until 1960.

With lengthy and heated debate over whether or not American ships should pay tolls, Congress finally ruled in 1914 that all ships, including American vessels, should pay the same toll, 90 cents per cargo ton. By law, the canal must break even financially, so when the Panama Canal Company (which had been operating the canal since 1914) had its first loss in 1973, rates were raised to $1.08 per cargo ton the following year. Since then the tolls have been raised three more times, with the *Queen Elizabeth II* paying the highest toll on record in 1988, $106,782.33 and 140-pound adventurer Richard Halliburton paying the lowest toll when he swam the canal for 36 cents in 1928. Although supertankers and the U.S. Navy's supercarriers are too large to make the transit, at least twenty percent of the more than 12,000 ships that go through the canal annually are PANAMAX size. With a maximum width of 106 feet and a maximum length of 950 feet, PANAMAX ships are the largest vessels that the locks can handle.

Over the years, the Panama Canal has not only had a positive impact on world trade and commerce but on the Republic of Panama as well. In addition to the many millions of dollars that have been paid to Panama by the United States for use of the canal, U.S. military forces stationed in Panama, as well as canal employees, have generated a demand for goods and services that has boosted Panama's economy.

But there has been a negative impact too. Tensions between the United States and Panama go all the way back to the 1903 Hay–Bunau-Varilla Treaty, which literally split the Isthmus in two and gave the United States what Panamanians considered near-colonial rights in the middle of their country. John Hay, the American Secretary of State who signed the treaty, even admitted in a letter to a senator that the treaty was "vastly advantageous to the United States, and we must confess, with what face we can muster, not so advantageous to Panama. . . . You and I know too well how many points there are in this treaty to which a Panamanian patriot could object."

Distrust between American workers and Panamanian citizens existed from the beginning. "In temperament and tradition we are miles away from the Panamanians," observed a magazine correspondent. "Differences in language, customs and religious practices keep the breach wide," wrote another, while official statements over the years have done little to ease the tension. In 1909 President Taft pointed out that the United States had rights in the Zone as if sovereign while Panama had none. "Now that may be a ticklish argument; but I do not care whether it is nor not," he said. "We are there. We have the right to govern that strip, and we are going to govern it."

Believing that the Panamanians were lazy as well as not properly grateful for everything being done for them, Americans called all Panamanians, from a market woman on the street to an educated professional, "Spiggotty" or "Spig," an insulting term supposedly derived from Panamanian hack drivers calling out to customers that they could "speaka-da-English."

"The strongest quality of the Panamanian is his pride, and it is precisely that sentiment which we North Americans have either wantonly or necessarily outraged," Willis Abbot wrote. Dr. William Gorgas was one of the few on the canal staff who could speak Spanish, while Colonel Goethals, who spent seven years on the Isthmus as chief engineer and almost three as Zone governor, never even tried to learn.

When the Commission began to provide all food and supplies to American workers at near cost in 1906, the decision not only violated the 1903 treaty but also deprived Panamanian merchants of the profits they had been promised. As for sanitation, Panamanians angrily pointed out that they had managed to live for centuries without fumigating their buildings with foul-smelling concoctions or spraying oil on their brooks, streams and ponds, not to mention on their churches' baptismal water. Offended by what they perceived to be American arrogance, Panamanians, in turn, contemptuously labeled Americans "gringoes."

Under the terms of the 1903 treaty, the United States was entitled to "the use, occupation and control of any other lands and waters outside the zone" that might be "necessary and convenient" for the running of the canal. Over the years, those terms have seen Panama, a small country to begin with, lose more than 200 square miles of territory as the Canal Zone increased in size from its original 436 square miles to 647 square miles.

Another source of bitterness was that the rising waters of Gatun Lake forced thousands of native Panamanians to move from villages where their ancestors had lived for centuries. Major Sibert

(Right) The natives' flimsy shacks are no match for the Commission's heavy equipment.

apparently never understood the Panamanian point of view. He complained, "It was, in many cases, necessary to forcibly remove the inhabitants. They could not appreciate, understand, or accept the proposed changes." Other Panamanian buildings were torn down by the Sanitary Department. In 1910, the *Canal Record* reported, "One hundred and fifty-two buildings were ordered destroyed by the Health Services. The work of removing the unsanitary houses and shacks is practically completed."

Predictably, serious trouble erupted even before the canal was finished. In 1912 three Marines were killed when a riot exploded in Panama City between Panamanian police and American Marines celebrating the Fourth of July. Three years later there was another riot, followed by more riots in 1947, 1958, 1959, 1962, 1968 and 1987, with one of the worst riots occurring in January, 1964, when four American soldiers and twenty-four Panamanians were killed, with hundreds more wounded after four days of vicious street fighting. The government of Panama raised charges of American brutality, breaking off diplomatic relations with the

United States for three months. In almost every instance of rioting, the trouble was caused by Panamanian frustration over American control in the Zone "as if it were sovereign," that phrase in the original treaty that has stuck like a bone in the throat of Panamanians since 1903.

It's not as if there haven't been new treaties. In both 1936 and 1955 the United States and Panama signed treaties that granted Panama more sovereignty in the Zone, including the right to fly the Panamanian and American flags jointly, a particularly prickly issue. In the 1936 treaty, at Panama's request, the United States withdrew its guarantee of Panamanian independence. Both treaties also increased annual payments to Panama for American use of the canal, while hiring practices and salaries of Panamanians working in the Zone were upgraded.

President Jimmy Carter and General Torrijos of Panama shake hands after signing two landmark treaties, September 7, 1977.

And then, on September 7, 1977, all earlier treaties were cancelled when two historic treaties were signed in Washington, D.C. between President Jimmy Carter and Panamanian Chief of Government Brigadier General Omar Torrijos, the result of more than twelve years of negotiations. After two-to-one approval by Panamanian voters and after the United States Senate gave its advice and consent to ratification (following the second longest treaty debate in United States history), the treaties went into effect on October 1, 1979.

On that date, the Panama Canal Treaty basically disbanded the Panama Canal Zone and its government, which had owned, operated and maintained the canal, the Panama Railroad, commissaries, workers' homes and all the utilities in the Zone. The railroad and sixty-five percent of Zone land were turned over to Panama, as well as shops, fueling facilities and warehouses. Panama also assumed responsibility for ship passengers, the police, the courts, commercial ship repairs and supplies, as well as railway and pier operations. The Panama Canal Company was replaced by the Panama Canal Commission, which manages, operates and maintains the canal under the supervision of a board made up of five Americans and four Panamanians, with an American serving as senior officer for the first ten years of the treaty and a Panamanian for the last ten years. With the transit zone, as it is now called, gradually reverting to Panama, more and more Panamanians are filling canal jobs; in 1988, eighty-four percent of the 8,000 Commission employees were Panamanian.

The treaty expires at noon on December 31, 1999, at which time the United States will turn over all rights and properties of the Panama Canal to Panama. After that date, no other nation but Panama may operate the canal or maintain military installations within Panama, although the United States has the right to use military force, if necessary, to keep the canal open.

Under the terms of the second treaty, the Neutrality Treaty, Panama and the United States guarantee the permanent neutrality of the canal, with equal access and tolls for all nations' merchant and naval vessels. U.S. and Panamanian warships will have the right of prompt and speedy passage through the canal at all times.

In 1986, a three-nation commission consisting of Japanese, Panamanian and American members began a five-year study of possible alternatives to the Panama Canal. They will consider the possibility of building a new sea-level canal, adding more locks to the existing canal, finding new ways to move equipment and goods across the Isthmus by land or continuing with the canal as it is now.

Of course there are continuing problems, controversy and disagreements. There always have been and probably always will be. How could there not be problems and controversy involving a project that has affected world shipping and trade for most of the twentieth century? But no matter what the future holds, nothing can detract from what the canal is, a passageway that not only links the Atlantic and Pacific, but also links the present to the past, the culmination of a dream that began when Balboa sighted the Pacific more than four and a half centuries ago. The Panama Canal was, and is, a living monument to its builders, to their engineering genius, to their victory over disease, but most of all, to the dedication and courage of their human spirit.

BIBLIOGRAPHY

Abbot, Willis J. *Panama and the Canal in Picture and Prose.* New York: Syndicate Publishing Company, 1913.

Avery, Ralph Emmett. *The Greatest Engineering Feat in the World at Panama.* New York: Leslie-Judge Company, 1915.

Biesanz, John and Mavis. *The People of Panama.* New York: Columbia University Press, 1955.

Bigelow, Poultney. "Our Mismanagement at Panama." *The Independent,* Volume 60 (New York, January 4, 1906), p. 12ff.

Bishop, Joseph Bucklin. *Notes and Anecdotes of Many Years.* New York: Charles Scribner's Sons, 1925.

————. *The Panama Gateway.* New York: Charles Scribner's Sons, 1915.

————. *Panama, Past and Present.* New York: The Century Company, 1913.

————, ed. *Theodore Roosevelt and His Time: Shown in His Own Letters.* New York: Charles Scribner's Sons, Volume 23, 1926.

————, ed. *Theodore Roosevelt's Letters to His Children.* New York: Charles Scribner's Sons, 1923.

————and Farnum Bishop. *Goethals: Genius of the Panama Canal.* New York: Harper and Brothers, 1930.

Bradford, Earle. *Christopher Columbus.* New York: The Viking Press, 1973.

Canal Record. Mount Hope, Canal Zone: Isthmian Canal Commission Printing Office, Volumes I–VIII, 1907–1915.

Carpenter, Allan. *Panama, Enchantment of Central America.* Chicago: Regensteiner Publishing Enterprises, Inc., 1971.

Cobb, Charles E. "Panama, Ever at the Crossroads." *National Geographic Magazine,* Vol. 169, No. 4, (April 1986), p. 466ff.

"Competition for the Best True Stories of Life and Work on the Isthmus of Panama During the Construction of the Panama Canal," Isthmian Historical Society, 1963.

DuVal, Miles P., Jr. *Cadiz to Cathay.* Stanford University, California: Stanford University Press, 1940.

Earle, Peter. *The Sack of Panama.* New York: The Viking Press, 1981.

Executive Orders Relating to the Panama Canal. Mount Hope, Canal Zone: The Panama Canal Printers, 1921.

Foster, Roman J. *Diggers.* New York: Diggers Productions, Inc., 1985.

Franck, Harry A. *Zone Policeman 88.* New York: The Century Company, 1913.

Goethals, George W. "The Panama Canal." *National Geographic Magazine.* Vol. 22, No. 2 (February 1911), p. 148ff.

―――, ed. *The Panama Canal: An Engineering Treatise.* New York: McGraw-Hill Book Company, Inc., 1916, Volumes I and II.

Gorgas, Marie D. and Burton J. Hendrick. *William Crawford Gorgas: His Life and Work.* Garden City, N.Y.: Doubleday, Doran and Company, Inc., 1935.

Gorgas, William Crawford. "Health Conditions in the Canal Zone." *Harper's Weekly,* Volume 49, No. 2527. (May 27, 1905).

―――. *Report of the Department of Sanitation of the Isthmian Canal Commission for the Month of March, 1914.* Washington, D.C., 1914.

―――. *Sanitation in Panama.* New York and London: D. Appleton and Company, 1915.

Hagedorn, Hermann, ed. *The Works of Theodore Roosevelt: State Papers as Governor and President, 1899–1909.* New York: Charles Scribner's Sons, 1925.

Haskin, Frederic J. *The Panama Canal.* Garden City, NY: Doubleday, Page and Company, 1913.

Howarth, David. *Panama, 400 Years of Dreams and Cruelty.* New York: McGraw-Hill Book Company, 1966.

Keen, Benjamin, translator and annotator. *The Life of the Admiral Christopher Columbus by His Son Ferdinand.* New Brunswick, N.J.: Rutgers University Press, 1959.

Klette, Immanuel. *From Atlantic to Pacific.* New York: Harper and Row, 1967.

LaFeber, Walter. *The Panama Canal: The Crisis in Historical Perspective.* New York: Oxford University Press, 1978.

Lee, W. Storrs. *The Strength to Move a Mountain.* New York: G. P. Putnam's Sons, 1958.

Letters Transmitting the Report of the Board of Consulting Engineers for the Panama Canal. Washington, D.C.: Washington Government Printing Office, 1906.

"Life on the Canal Zone." *The Independent*, Volume 60, (New York, March 22, 1906), p. 656ff.

Lindsay, Forbes. *Panama and the Canal To-Day.* Boston: L.C. Page and Company, 1912.

Liss, Sheldon, B. *The Canal.* London: University of Notre Dame Press, 1967.

Lyle, Eugene P., Jr. "The Real Conditions at Panama." *The World's Work*, (New York: Doubleday Page and Company, November 1905), p. 6875ff.

Mack, Gerstle. *The Land Divided: A History of the Panama Canal and Other Isthmian Projects.* New York: Alfred A. Knopf, 1944.

Maltby, Frank B. "In at the Start at Panama." *Civil Engineering*, (June, July, August, September 1945),: p. 260ff., 322ff., 360ff., 421ff.

McCullough, David. *The Path Between the Seas: The Creation of the Panama Canal 1870–1914.* New York: Simon and Schuster, 1977.

Message of the President of the United States Communicated to the Two Houses of Congress on January 4, 1904. Washington: Government Printing Office, 1904.

Morison, Elting E., ed. *The Letters of Theodore Roosevelt.* Cambridge, Mass.: Harvard University Press, 1951, Volumes 3 and 4.

Official Handbook of the Panama Canal, 1915. Washington, D.C.: Washington Government Printing Office, 1915.

"Oldtimers Well Remember the Yellow Peril." *The Panama Canal Review*, (April 2, 1954), p. 8ff.

Otis, Fessenden Nott. *Illustrated History of the Panama Railroad.* New York: Harper and Brothers, 1862.

The Panama Canal, Twenty-fifth Anniversary, August 15, 1914. Balboa Heights, Canal Zone, 1939.

The Panama Canal, Fiftieth Anniversary, 1914–1964. Panama Canal Information Office, La Boca, Canal Zone, 1964.

Panama Canal Commission. Official Brochures, Publications, Advisories, Biographical Material, Fiscal Statistics, Press Releases. Balboa, Panama.

Panama Star and Herald. Vol. 7 (July 30, 1905), pp. 13, 689, Vol. 59 (March 1, 1907), pp. 14, 193; Vol. 59 (March 19, 1907), pp. 14, 193.

Parker, Elizabeth Kittredge. *Panama Canal Bride.* New York: Exposition Press, 1955.

Pennell, Joseph. *Joseph Pennell's Pictures of the Panama Canal.* Philadelphia: J. B. Lippincott Company, 1912.

Pepperman, Walter Leon. *Who Built the Panama Canal?* New York: E. P. Dutton and Company, 1915.

"Pictorial History of Canal Construction." *The Panama Canal Review,* (April 2, 1954), p. 9ff.

Pringle, Henry F. *Theodore Roosevelt: A Biography.* New York: Harcourt, Brace and Company, 1931.

"Proceedings." Isthmian Canal Commission. Meetings, No. 1–49 (March 1904 to September 1904).

"Reminiscences of Thirty-Five Old Timers Who Helped Dig the Panama Canal." Isthmian Historical Society. Roosevelt Medal-Holders' Tape-Recorder Guest Book (November 17, 1958).

Robinson, Tracy. *Fifty Years at Panama.* New York: The Trow Press, 1907.

Roosevelt, Theodore. *An Autobiography.* New York: Charles Scribner's Sons, 1925.

Scofield, John. "Christopher Columbus and the New World He Found." *National Geographic Magazine,* Vol. 148, No. 5 (November 1975), p. 584ff.

"The Sea-Level Versus the Lock Canal." *The Independent,* Volume 60, (New York, March 29, 1906), p. 709ff.

Sibert, William L. and John F. Stevens. *The Construction of the Panama Canal.* New York: D. Appleton and Company, 1915.

Simon, Maron J. *The Panama Affair.* New York: Charles Scribner's Sons, 1971.

Slosson, Edwin E. and Gardner Richardson. "The Independent's Report on Panama." *The Independent,* Volume 60, (New York, March 15, 1906), p. 592ff.

Stevens, John F. "Transactions." Paper #1650. *American Society of Civil Engineers.* New York, NY: July 13, 1927.

Syme, Ronald. *Balboa, Finder of the Pacific.* New York: William Morrow and Company, 1956.

United States Department of State. Unclassified Material on Panama and the Panama Canal, 1985, 1986, 1987.

Van Hardeveld, Rose. *Make the Dirt Fly!* Hollywood CA: The Pan Press, 1956.

Verrill, A. Hyatt. *Panama, Past and Present.* New York: Dodd, Mead and Company, 1921.

"The Week." *Nation.* Volume 77, No. 2003 and 2004, (November 19 and November 26, 1903), p. 212 and p. 398.

"What We Inherit with the Panama Canal." *Scientific American.* Vol. 91, No. 4 (July 23, 1904).

STATISTICS—PANAMA CANAL—1914

Panama Canal Zone—436 square miles

Chief Engineers:
John F. Wallace: June 1904—June 1905
John F. Stevens: July 1905—January 1907
George W. Goethals: February 1907—January 1914

Transit:
Length of Panama Canal from deep water to deep water—50 miles
Transit time—ten to twelve hours
Shortens distance from New York to San Francisco—7,873 miles
Deep water in the Atlantic to Limon Bay shoreline—4 miles—500 feet wide
Limon Bay shoreline to Gatun locks—3 miles—500 feet wide
Gatun Lake—164 square miles
Channel across Gatun Lake—24 miles—500 to 1,000 feet wide
Culebra Cut [Gaillard Cut]—9 miles—300 feet wide
Miraflores Lake—1.88 square miles
Channel across Miraflores Lake—1.5 miles—500 feet wide
Miraflores locks to Bay of Panama shoreline—4.5 miles—500 feet wide
Bay of Panama shoreline to deep water in the Pacific—4 miles—500 feet wide
Sea level channels—15.5 miles [salt water]
Elevated channels—34.5 miles [freshwater]
Each transiting ship uses 52 million gallons of fresh water.
Highest toll paid—*Queen Elizabeth II*—$106,782.33 (1988)
Lowest toll paid—swimmer Richard Halliburton—36 cents (1928)

Locks:

Gatun—three sets of locks—six chambers—lift 85 feet
Pedro Miguel—one set of locks—two chambers—lift 30 feet
Miraflores—two sets of locks—four chambers—lift 55 feet
Lock chamber:
    length—1,000 feet
    width—110 feet
    depth—70 to 80 feet
Approach wall—1,000 feet
Lock gates:
    total—46 [92 leaves]
    length of each leaf—65 feet
    height of each leaf—47 to 82 feet
    weight of each leaf—390 to 730 tons
    thickness of each leaf—7 feet
Culverts:
    main—18 feet in diameter
    cross—6.5 feet by 8 feet
    floor holes—4.5 feet in diameter

Dams:

Gatun Dam:
    length—1.5 miles
    width at base—.5 mile
    width at top—100 feet
    height above sea level—105 feet
    size—300 acres
    spillway dam:
      length—808 feet
      gates—14
      height of gates—115.5 feet above sea level
    spillway channel:
      length—1,200 feet
      width—285 feet
Miraflores spillway dam:
    length—500 feet
    gates—8

Breakwaters:

    Naos—length—3.26 miles
    Toro Point—length—2 miles

Total American excavation—232,440,945 cubic yards
Greatest number of employees—56,654 in 1913

INDEX

Page numbers in italics refer to photographs.

CREDITS

Quotes of West Indian workers excerpted from "Diggers," produced by Roman J. Foster, copyright © 1985 by Roman J. Foster.

Diagrams and maps on pages 2–3, 14, 49, 75, 89 and 102 are by Jeanyee Wong.

Photos

Jimmy Carter Library: p. 146
Library of Congress: pp. 12, 16, 28, 47, 54, 67, 110
National Archives: pp. 20, 22, 48, 64, 81, 85, 87, 97, 113, 120, 122, 123, 131, 132, 140
National Geographic: p. 118
Panama Canal Commission: pp. 4, 10, 17, 31, 34, 37, 43, 44, 51, 56, 60, 61, 63, 71, 72, 76, 80, 83, 84, 86, 91, 93, 95, 98, 105, 106, 107, 112 (top and bottom), 114, 115, 116, 117, 119, 124, 128, 133, 137, 138, 145